SOME QUESTIONNAIRE MEASURES OF EMPLOYEE MOTIVATION AND MORALE

A Report on Their Reliability and Validity

by

MARTIN PATCHEN

With the Collaboration of
Donald C. Pelz and Craig W. Allen

SURVEY RESEARCH CENTER

INSTITUTE FOR SOCIAL RESEARCH
THE UNIVERSITY OF MICHIGAN
ANN ARBOR, MICHIGAN

SOME QUESTIONNAIRE MEASURES OF EMPLOYEE MOTIVATION AND MORALE

A Report on Their Reliability and Validity

by

MARTIN PATCHEN

With the Collaboration of
Donald C. Pelz and Craig W. Allen

Survey Research Center
INSTITUTE FOR SOCIAL RESEARCH
The University of Michigan

ISR Code No. 2351

Library of Congress Catalog Card No. 65-65052
ISBN 0-87944-045-7

Published by the Survey Research Center
of the Institute for Social Research,
The University of Michigan, Ann Arbor, Michigan 48106

First Published 1965
Seventh Printing 1977

© 1965 by The University of Michigan, All Rights Reserved
Manufactured in the United States of America

To Lloyd L. Huntington

Who worked to encourage employee involvement in their jobs and saw the importance of measuring such qualities

ACKNOWLEDGEMENTS

The work reported in this monograph is part of a larger project concerned with the effects of different work environments on employee feelings of involvement with their jobs and their work organizations. The initial general planning of the project was done jointly by Donald C. Pelz, my senior colleague at the Survey Research Center, and myself. Dr. Pelz took an active part in the project's early phases — collaborating especially in the work of gaining entrance to the sites where we worked, in designing the method of getting supervisory judgments, and in actually collecting the data. His other commitments and the fact that he has spent the past year in India have prevented Dr. Pelz from taking part in the analysis and write-up of the results.

In the early phases of the project, I received invaluable help from Craig W. Allen, who served as Assistant Director of the project during its first year. Mr. Allen assisted me in doing exploratory interviewing, in writing the questionnaire items, in collecting data, and in early analysis of the data.

Susanna Y. Hubley did an excellent job in handling most of the clerical and typing duties of the first part of the project and also assisted in exploratory interviewing and pre-testing. Alison Clark performed additional clerical and computer work in the latter part of the data analysis; her skill in working with IBM equipment was a very great asset. Michael Brown assisted with the interviewing and data collection at the electronics company.

We are grateful to the management officials and union officers at the Tennessee Valley Authority for their cooperation in making the study possible. In particular, we are indebted to Lloyd L. Huntington, former staff officer of the Personnel Division at TVA, who first interested us in TVA, who physically and verbally guided us through TVA's complex organization, and who served as a liason between us and TVA people. We are grateful also to the management of the electronics company which also participated in the study for their general cooperation and for their effort to provide us with the information and help we needed. Finally, I wish to thank Dr. David G. Bowers of the Survey Research Center for using one of the measures we developed in his study of an appliance company and for permission to use some of the data he gathered.

The project was supported by a research grant (No. M4514) from the National Institutes of Health. We are greatly appreciative of this support.

While acknowledging the valuable contributions of others to this report, the sole responsibility for the final product is my own.

July 1965   Martin Patchen

CONTENTS

	Page
Acknowledgements	iii
I. BACKGROUND AND PURPOSES	1
II. THE SITES AND SAMPLES	4
Organizational Units Included	4
General Description of Units	4
Employee-Management Relations	6
Sampling Within Major Sites	6
Summary	8
III. METHODS OF DEVELOPING MEASURES	9
General Approach	9
Preparation of Items	9
Pre-tests of Questionnaires	9
Questionnaire Administration	10
Selection of Items	10
Validating Data	11
Reliability	13
Summary	14
IV. INTEREST IN WORK INNOVATION INDEX	15
Questionnaire Items	15
Reliability	16
Correlation Among Items	16
Relation to Supervisors' Rankings	17
Relation to Suggestions	20
Relation to Other Variables	23
Summary and Conclusions	24
V. JOB MOTIVATION INDICES	26
Questionnaire Items	26
Reliability	27
Correlation Among Items	27
Relation to Supervisors' Rankings	28
Relation to Absence	30
Relation to Productive Efficiency	33
Comparison of Occupational Groups	35

	Relation to Other Variables	36
	Summary and Conclusions	37
VI.	ACCEPTANCE OF JOB CHANGES INDEX	40
	Questionnaire Items	40
	Reliability	41
	Correlation Among Items	42
	Relation to Supervisors' Rankings	42
	Relation to Other Variables	44
	Summary and Conclusions	47
VII.	WILLINGNESS TO DISAGREE WITH SUPERVISORS INDEX	48
	Questionnaire Items	48
	Reliability	49
	Correlation Among Items	49
	Relation to Supervisors' Rankings	50
	Relation to Other Variables	52
	Summary and Conclusions	54
VIII.	IDENTIFICATION WITH THE WORK ORGANIZATION INDICES	55
	Questionnaire Items	55
	Reliability	58
	Correlation Among Items	60
	Relation to Supervisors' Rankings	61
	Relation to Displaying an Organization Sticker	62
	Relation to Turnover	65
	Relation to Expectation of Remaining with Organization	66
	Relation to Length of Service	68
	Relation to Attendance	68
	Relation to Other Variables	68
	Summary and Conclusions	69
IX.	OVERALL EVALUATION OF THE MEASURES	71
APPENDICES	73
REFERENCES	81

I. BACKGROUND AND PURPOSES

For several decades, social scientists and practitioners have been assessing the attitudes of people in organizations, especially business organizations. A great many different questions have been asked of employees concerning their job satisfaction, job interest, feeling toward the organization, attitudes toward changes in the work situation, and so on. The kind of information derived from such questions is important to those responsible for organizational decisions and they have sometimes used such information as an aid. Employee answers to questions concerning their morale and motivation have also been used by social scientists in their efforts to understand better the determinants of motivation and satisfaction on the job.

It is not always clear, however, how reliable and how valid are the data concerning morale and motivation which is obtained from interviews or questionnaires administered to employees. The problem of the validity of a question is, of course, the problem of whether it is actually measuring what it is supposed to measure. Almost always the users of questionnaires have relied on "face validity" — the fact that the items appear to be appropriate ones. Yet we know that a face-valid item may lack validity by more stringent standards (American Psychological Association, 1954). There are many reasons why this may be so. The item may simply not be understood by the respondent correctly; it may be eliciting answers which are too heavily colored by social desirability; it may be getting at a dimension different from the one it is intended to get at; or it may not be sensitive enough to real differences.

The reliability of any measure is, of course, its consistency in giving the same "reading" — e.g., in giving the same results tomorrow as it does today. As with validity, it is not at all self-evident that any given question, or set of questions, will give reliable results. There may be random error in responses; there may be changes in the meaning communicated by the question; the attitudes tapped may be uncrystallized or volatile.

Psychologists have given considerable attention to the reliability and validity of some questionnaire measurements. However, work of this kind has been done primarily for tests of personality characteristics. Characteristics such as the tendency to seek affiliation, to be dominant, and to try to achieve, have been measured and evidence concerning the reliability and validity of such measures has been offered (e.g. Edwards, 1959; Gough, 1957; Ghiselli, 1963). While such questionnaire measures may be quite useful in trying to predict an individual's attitudes and behavior on the job, they are clearly not measures of his actual work attitudes in a specific situation.

Some measurement work more directly concerned with the job situation has been done with respect to job satisfaction. A group of researchers at the Industrial Relations Center of the University of Minnesota has developed questionnaire measures of five components of job satisfaction (Carlson, et. al., 1962). They indicate that the items within each of the scales are intercorrelated and that the scales are, for the most part, highly reliable and independent. Patricia Smith and her colleagues at Cornell have also developed questionnaire measures by administering to the same employees both questionnaire measures and several verbal and non-verbal rating scales of satisfaction, and then comparing the results (Macauley et. al., 1963). Relevant work has been done also by Roach (1958), Decker (1955), and Campbell and Tyler (1957).

Aside from the measurement of job satisfaction, there have been very few attempts to develop reliable and valid measures of attitudes on the job. One such measure is a scale of "job involvement" very recently developed by Lodahl and Kejner (In Press). This scale is composed of items which bear on such things as concern about one's work, sense of duty in work, tendencies to avoid coming to work, and the felt importance of one's work. This "job involvement" scale has a satisfactory reliability and is related to several job factors, such as perceived chance for promotion and frequent contacts with others on the job. The scale is, however, not related to some other job factors to which it was expected to relate and there is not as yet direct evidence of its relation to actual behavior which might reflect high job involvement.

Another relevant measurement effort is the work of Mahoney (1956). He developed unidimensional scales of nine aspects of "morale," including attitudes toward leadership at several levels, feeling of belongingness at work, and feelings of the extent of sacrifice at work. He reports acceptable internal-consistency reliabilities for his scales and shows the questionnaire-derived scales to have moderate correlations with ratings based on interviews. Though scores on several of Mahoney's scales (though not feelings of the Extent of Sacrifice on the Job) are correlated with ratings of performance and with attendance, his work has the limitation that the same external criteria are used to help establish the validity of the different scales.

Our own immediate concern with the measurement of employee motivation and morale grew out of a larger project in which we have been studying some of the determinants of employee involvement in their jobs. The available measures of employee attitudes did not tap the specific aspects of motivation and morale in which we were most interested. While the measurement of employee attitudes toward their jobs was not our main goal, we felt the need of evaluating the reliability of the measures to be used in our analysis. We therefore built into our data-gathering operations some procedures for trying to establish the validity and reliability of our measures.

The specific employee characteristics with which we have been most concerned are the following:

BACKGROUND AND PURPOSES

1. Job motivation: level of aroused motivation on the job.
2. Interest in work innovation: in finding new ways of doing things on the job.
3. Willingness to express disagreement with supervisors.
4. Attitude toward changes introduced into the job situation.
5. Identification with the work organization.

For each of these five characteristics, we evaluated the reliability and validity of questionnaire items intended to be an indicator of that characteristic. We then combined the best items bearing on each characteristic to form an index measure of that characteristic.

This monograph is a report of the methods we used and the results obtained in developing these measures. The measures were intended primarily for use in our own work and each has a smaller number of items than might be optimally desirable.[1] However, the evidence concerning the reliability and validity of these measures is sufficiently encouraging to warrant making them available to others. Therefore, while recognizing their limitations, we are presenting this report in the hope that the measures may prove useful to others — both researchers and practitioners — who are concerned with employee motivation and morale.

In the next section, we describe the sites and samples used for the study. Section 3 outlines the methods used for developing the measures and assessing their validity and reliability. Sections 4 through 8 describe in turn each of the five motivation and morale measures and the evidence bearing on their usefulness. Section 9 briefly evaluates the measures presented and makes some suggestions concerning the conditions under which they may be most useful.

---

[1] However, since each Likert-type item is itself a small scale, it appears that not as many items are needed as where dichotomous questions are used.

II. THE SITES AND SAMPLES

The present study was done primarily in five geographically separate units of the Tennessee Valley Authority and in a private electronics company. TVA is a semi-autonomous part of the United States government devoted to overall development of the Tennessee Valley through electric power production, flood control, agricultural improvement, and other services. The electronics company manufactures communications products for both consumers and government. Supplementary data, on the measure of job motivation only, were obtained from a company which manufactures household appliances.[1]

Organizational Units Included

At TVA the following units were included in the study: Division of Design, Knoxville, Tenn.; Division of Power Planning and Engineering, Chattanooga, Tenn.; Gallatin Steam Plant, Gallatin, Tenn.; John Sevier Steam Plant, Rogersville, Tenn.; and Johnsonville Steam Plant, Johnsonville, Tenn.

In the electronics company, three divisions — each making different products — were included, along with several units at the corporate level. These divisions are all in a major Northern metropolitan area but are geographically separated by several miles. In the appliance company, data were obtained from the five major departments of the company. These departments are all located in a small midwestern town.

General Description of Units

TVA Engineering Divisions. One of the two TVA Engineering divisions studied, the Division of Design, produces the blueprints for the major new construction jobs of TVA — steam plants, dams, etc. The division employs about 600 persons — most of them civil, mechanical, and electrical engineers. Other occupations represented include architects and draftsmen. The work is fairly highly specialized — according to the type of installation and the aspect of construction being planned. For example, within the Electrical Design branch, there are units which specialize in steam plant switchboard design and in hydro plant conduit and grounding design.

Basic work units are fairly small — groups of two to twenty men,

---

[1] Data from the appliance company were obtained as part of a study directed by David G. Bowers and Kurt Student. They included in their questionnaire the measure of general job motivation developed at the other sites. These data are presented in the section concerning the job motivation measure.

with the average about nine men. There is considerable communication among men in different units working on complementary parts of a structure and some shifting of men across units from time to time. The division works under demanding time deadlines.

The second TVA engineering division covered is the Division of Power Planning and Engineering. Whereas the Division of Design plans major installations like a steam plant, this division designs facilities which carry the power, including transmission lines and sub-stations. Of five branches in the division, two are concerned primarily with future planning, rather than with designs for immediate construction. The occupations and the work organization in this division are generally similar to that described for the Division of Design. The two divisions are, however, administratively separate. The Division of Power Planning employs about 300 persons.

<u>TVA Steam Plants.</u> The three steam plants studied are part of a complex of fifteen TVA steam plants. They produce electricity by converting coal to steam which powers giant electric generators. Each plant has an almost identical technology and administrative structure. The operating section of each plant is responsible for checking and guiding the operation of a largely automated complex of equipment. The work of the operators and their assistants centers around control rooms where a set of dials, lights, and other indicators shows the conditions in various parts of the plant. The job of the mechanical and electrical maintenance sections is to maintain and repair the plant's equipment. These sections are composed of machinists, boilermakers, steamfitters, electricians, and other craftsmen. The laboratory section of each plant samples and tests the coal which is brought into the plant as well as doing other analytic and testing work. Each plant operates around the clock. Operating personnel work on rotating shifts. The day-to-day operations of each plant are largely under the control of its superintendent, but the plants are coordinated by a central office in Chattanooga.

<u>Electronics Firm.</u> In each of the three electronics divisions, at least two types of units, an engineering unit and a production unit, were included. The three engineering units are composed mainly of electrical engineers and draftsmen. The engineers design products such as auto radios. Sometimes they work on a problem in small groups of two or three; other times an individual engineer works on a problem himself.

Production workers are almost entirely women — most of them with families and working for extra income. Some of them work on products which move along on an assembly line. Almost all do work which requires close attention and manual dexterity in such tasks as wiring and soldering electrical equipment. Standard production rates are set for most jobs and pressures are exerted on employees to "make the rates."

A single sales unit covered in the study is composed of salesmen who have a good deal of independence in handling a geographical territory in which they sell to firms rather than to individual consumers. Some of the salesmen themselves have subordinates. Employees in finance, purchasing, and marketing units are primarily male and do various kinds of clerical and administrative work.

Appliance Firm. The greatest number of employees in the appliance company work along moving assembly lines. Other sizable groups of employees work in machine shops and in sheet metal shops. These shops do the stamping of parts, lathe work, grinding work, and other operations necessary to provide the parts which are put together on the assembly lines. Almost nine out of ten employees are male.

Employee-Management Relations

TVA. Most TVA employees included in the study are represented by employee organizations. In the engineering divisions, most of the employees are members of the TVA Engineers Association, which acts as a bargaining agent with management. Some employees in the engineering divisions are members of an office worker's union which includes both TVA and non-TVA members. Most of the employees studied in the steam plants are members of international AFL-CIO craft unions, while a few belong to other employee organizations, such as the Engineers Association.

Union-management relations at TVA have been, for the most part, cordial and even friendly. There is, moreover, in each of the sites studied, a conference system whereby once a month employee and management representatives meet to discuss work problems outside the scope of the formal union contract. In each steam plant, there are two conferences, one for "white collar" employees (primarily laboratory and administrative) and one for other employees.

Electronics Company. There are no unions representing employees at the electronics company. Management has opposed unionization, and a union attempt to organize production workers, several years prior to our study, failed. Wages were slightly higher than in other companies in the industry. The company also has a profit-sharing plan paying substantial benefits to employees when they retire.

Appliance Company. Employees at the appliance company are represented by a strong national union. Relations between union and management, while not overly warm, are generally amicable. There has been no strike in over a decade. Most employees have an opportunity to earn extra incentive pay, on the basis either of their individual output or that of their group.

Sampling Within Major Sites

TVA. Within the Division of Design, approximately half of the non-supervisory employees stationed at Knoxville were asked to take the questionnaire. In the larger work sections (seven persons or more), every other name on the organization personnel list was chosen. In the smaller work sections (six or under), every other section doing similar work was chosen.[2] Of those chosen to take the questionnaire, 95% actually filled it out.

In the Division of Power Planning and Engineering, a smaller division, all non-supervisory employees stationed at Chattanooga were asked to take questionnaires. 98% of those asked filled out questionnaires.

In each steam plant, all non-supervisory employees in the mechanical maintenance, laboratory, and electrical maintenance sections were asked to take the questionnaire. Those in a portion of the operating section — that portion which is responsible for the actual operation of the equipment — were also included. Persons in that part of the operating section who do work in the "yard" were omitted. These men are mostly unskilled or semi-skilled, including janitors, heavy equipment operators, and laborers. One reason for their being omitted was that pre-tests indicated that these poorly-schooled men had some trouble understanding the questionnaire. Persons in the administrative section of each steam plant were also omitted from the study. Response rates to the questionnaire were 84% at Gallatin Steam Plant, 87% at John Sevier Steam Plant, and 88% at Johnsonville Steam Plant. Nonrespondents included absentees, those on vacations and leaves of absence, and those who missed a questionnaire administration session and then did not mail back the form left for them. For all of TVA, 834 employees completed the questionnaire.

Electronics Company. In some units of the electronics company, all employees were asked to take the questionnaire. In other departments —particularly some production departments — employees were chosen by management on the basis of their availability and the presence of production records for them. Since we were not especially concerned with describing the entire company population, it was not essential to have a completely random sample. In all, 223 employees in the electronics company completed the questionnaire.

Appliance Company. In the appliance company, almost all employees in the major departments were included in the sample. The median response rate in those units included in the analysis was 78%; the total number of employees completing the questionnaire was 557. Some of those choosing not to take the questionnaire were influenced by a vocal former union official who maintained that the study might be against the men's interests. However, the union itself supported the study.

---

[2] This method of sampling was adopted in order to ensure that there would be enough employees from every section represented so that a mean score on certain variables could be computed.

Summary

The study of which the measurement effort was a part was done primarily at five geographically separate units of the Tennessee Valley Authority and in several divisions of a private electronics company. Supplementary data on one of the measures was obtained at an appliance firm. Many different types of employees were covered. These include engineers in several specialities, operating personnel in automated power plants, clerical employees, salesmen, and semi-skilled production workers.

III. METHODS OF DEVELOPING MEASURES

General Approach

The basic method used in developing the measures was essentially what has come to be called the "empirical technique" (Gough, 1957). Questionnaire items to be included in a measure were chosen primarily on the basis of the validity evidence for each item — especially according to whether responses to the question were related to evidence of actual behavior. The empirical approach has been used before by others (e.g., Ghiselli, 1954; Gough, 1957).

This approach differs from the method whereby items are chosen essentially according to their relation to other items intended to measure the same characteristic (e.g. Lodahl and Kejner, In Press) and by which evidence for the validity of the measure is sought only after the items have been chosen.

The empirical method used in our own study has both advantages and disadvantages. Its main advantage is, of course, the greater assurance that the measures developed will be related to actual behavior. The major disadvantage is that each measure developed may not be "pure" — in the sense that it may contain items which measure somewhat different things.

Preparation of Items

Before the questionnaire items were written, informal interviews were conducted with approximately 25 supervisory employees and approximately 50 non-supervisory employees in various parts of TVA. Questions were thus constructed with some knowledge of the job situations of employees in many different types of work. Most of the items used were written for the present study. Some were adapted from items used in previous Survey Research Center studies. The questionnaire items intended to measure each of several aspects of morale and motivation are presented in the section which discusses that characteristic.

Pre-tests of Questionnaires

Two pre-tests were conducted at TVA. In each case, employees in one engineering organization and one steam plant were asked to fill out questionnaires. The first pre-test included 40 employees; the second covered 66 employees. These pre-tests were used to eliminate or revise questions which were inappropriate, misunderstood, or which had a poor "spread" in response distribution.

A questionnaire nearly identical to that used at TVA was later pretested with 60 employees of the electronics company. A number of informal interviews were also conducted. The preliminary work indicated that most questions could be used again in the electronics company. A few questions were revised for use at the electronics company.

Questionnaire Administration

Questionnaires were administered at TVA in April, 1962 and at the electronics company in January, 1963. These questionnaires included items bearing on many other aspects of the job (e.g., exact nature of work, relation to peers, promotion chances) in addition to those relevant to morale and motivation. Employees had, about a week before administration, received individual letters from the University of Michigan staff explaining the purposes and procedures of the study. They were assembled in groups of 30 to 70. These sessions were during working hours, except for some operating employees in the steam plants who met after or before their work shift, but who were paid for their time. A University of Michigan representative again described the study and answered questions before employees filled out the questionnaires. Management persons were not present during these sessions.

Employees were assured of the complete confidentiality of their individual answers. They were informed prior to taking the questionnaire that a code number identifying them — in order to match their answers with other information about them — would be placed on their questionnaires when they were finished. They were assured that these code numbers would be seen only by the University people. With only a few isolated exceptions, the explanation of the code system and its confidentiality seemed to have been accepted.

Mail-back questionnaires, to be completed either at work or at home, were left for the few persons who were unable to attend the group sessions. Most of these were filled out and returned.

The conditions of questionnaire administration at the appliance company were essentially similar except that individual respondents were completely anonymous, even to the researchers.

Selection of Items

For each employee characteristic we were attempting to measure, we began with a number of items which were thought to be potential indicators of that characteristic. Because we were also using the questionnaire to gather data about features of the job situation which might affect motivation and morale, the number of items in our initial pool for measuring each characteristic was limited (to about eight to ten items for each of the five characteristics to be measured).

Following pre-tests, we examined the relation between each of the questionnaire items and available validating evidence (described in the next section). Items which did not appear to discriminate individuals on the basis of the validity evidence were dropped. Other items were added for later pre-tests and/or for the final questionnaire administrations. A total of about fifty-five to sixty items were tried at one time or another.

Any item was accepted or rejected for inclusion in one of the indices primarily on the basis of whether it was successful in discriminating among employees according to available validity evidence. Other criteria for inclusion or noninclusion of an item were its test-retest reliability and its degree of association with other items intended to measure the same characteristic.

Validating Data

The proper meaning of "validity" for psychological measures has been subject to much debate in the literature (Bechtoldt, 1959; Campbell, 1960; Ebel, 1961). There have been, also, some differences in the terminology used by various writers.

Several types of validity distinguished by writers on the subject seem appropriate for establishing the usefulness of the measures with which we are concerned. These are convergent validity (Campbell and Fiske, 1959), construct validity (American Psychological Association, 1954), validation by known groups (Cronbach and Meehl, 1955), and the study of the inter-relation of items (Cronbach and Meehl, 1955). The major evidence relevant to each of these types of validity is outlined next.

A. <u>Convergent Validity.</u> This type of validation is "a confirmation by independent measurement procedures" (Campbell and Fiske, 1959).

1. <u>Ranking by Supervisory Judges.</u> A major measure used to try to establish convergent validity for each questionnaire measure is a pooled judgment of supervisors about each person with respect to the characteristic being measured.

    In ten organizational units at TVA and six units at the electronics company, five to ten supervisors were asked to meet. Each group was composed of first-line supervisors of the employees who took the questionnaire, plus any second-line supervisors, staff persons, or supervisors from other sections who were likely to know those who took the questionnaire.

    The purposes of the study and the confidentiality of the data were explained to the supervisors. The meaning of each of the qualities was explained, and a discussion about each quality was conducted to encourage the supervisors to think of concrete examples of how each quality might apply in their own unit's work. Next a deck of cards was passed to each supervisor, each bearing the name of a non-supervisory employee in that branch or section. Each supervisor was asked to keep the cards bearing the names of those persons whose work he knew by *personal* observation (not hearsay) and to discard the others. He was then asked to sort the names of those employees he knew into three or more (usually four) piles according to how they rank on the first quality; then to shuffle the cards and sort them into piles on the second quality; and so on. For any quality, the supervisor could put a man in a "can't rate" pile.

In scoring judges' rankings, a "ranking score" was given to an individual on a quality only if two or more persons ranked him on that quality and if the judges showed some degree of consensus in their judgments. (See Appendix B for further details of the scoring procedure).

The descriptions of each employee characteristic which were given to judges are noted in the separate sections concerning each characteristic. The forms on which the judges recorded their rankings are shown in Appendix A.

2. Suggestions. In attempting to validate items intended to measure interest in innovation, the questionnaire responses were related to data on number of suggestions made through official suggestion machinery. Counting the number of such suggestions made is another, though imperfect, way of gauging an employee's interest in innovation. This data is discussed in the section "Interest in Work Innovation Index."

3. Displaying TVA Sticker. In the section on measurement of identification with the work organization, questionnaire items are related to a probable behavioral indicator of identification — the use of a TVA sticker on one's car.

B. Construct Validity is evaluated by seeing to which other variables the quality being measured is related. In this way, its meaning can be better interpreted. Cronbach (1960) states, "The more fully and confidently a test can be interpreted, the greater its validity." Construct validity was evaluated primarily by use of the following data:

1. Attendance. Since job motivation was expected to be causally related to attendance, questionnaire items intended to measure job motivation were related to attendance data.

2. Turnover. Identification with the work organization was expected to be causally related to turnover. These data are described further in the section on the "Identification" measure.

3. Productivity. Measures of job motivation were related to data on productive efficiency.

4. Job Characteristics. Motivation and morale measures were also related to a number of aspects of the job situation — e.g., employee participation in decision-making, opportunities for achievement on the job — with which they might be expected to be causally associated.

C. Validation by Known Groups. In attempting to validate several of the measures, the method of validation by known groups (Cronbach and Meehl, 1955) is used. The principal use of this method is to compare several occupational groups known to differ in job motivation with respect to their scores on job motivation items.

D. Study of Correlations Among Items. Throughout the report, we examine correlations among items intended to measure the same characteristic. As Cronbach and Meehl (1955) point out, high intercorrelations are an indication of the validity of a measure when the logic of the construct calls for high correlations. In some cases, however, there is reason to expect that several aspects of the same characteristic will not be strongly correlated. For example, trying out new ideas on one's own and suggesting new ideas to a supervisor may both be aspects of interest in innovation, but we would not necessarily expect a high correlation between these behaviors. The degree of intercorrelation which might reasonably be expected was used to help evaluate the validity of marginal items. However, since we were not attempting to construct strictly uni-dimensional scales, items having low correlations with other items but good validity evidence of other kinds were sometimes included in an index.

In addition to the major validating evidence noted above, additional relevant evidence is introduced in the body of the report where appropriate.

It should be noted that we are not attempting to predict criterion measures of the characteristics we are attempting to measure. This is because there are no criteria available that "exemplify a measurement procedure clearly superior (i.e., more relevant and precise than) that embodied in the test" (Ebel, 1961). As Ebel points out, such criteria are usually not available, and in the case of some variables (like identification with the organization), real criterion measures probably do not exist. Since we rely on the other methods of validation outlined above, we cannot hope for magnitudes of correlation approaching 1.0, such as might be the goal when predicting to a good criterion measure.

Reliability

Test-retest reliability was assessed principally by re-administering the questionnaire to a group of 49 employees of the electronics company. A period of one month separated administrations. The re-administration was explained to respondents in terms of the fact that the second form "is different in many ways from the preliminary form and will also permit us to get some idea of your opinions as of the present moment." Supplementary data with which to assess reliability of questions relevant to identification with the work organization were available for 32 TVA employees at one engineering division.

Reliability coefficients were also computed for thirteen groups at the electronics company. The number of respondents in these groups (persons with the same supervisors) available for test-retest was much smaller (a median of three) than the size of all groups in the study (a median of about six). Also, eight of the thirteen groups available for reliability study came from the same department, which would reduce the amount of variation in scores among groups at any point in time. Because of these special characteristics, the test-retest reliability coefficients shown for these groups are probably an underestimate of the reliability of group scores in our total population of groups.

Summary

The basic method used in developing the measures is the "empirical method" by which items were chosen primarily according to whether responses to the items were related to evidence of actual behavior. Scores on the questionnaire measures were compared (as relevant) to ratings of employees by supervisors; to the number of suggestions submitted by employees; to the display by employees of an organizational auto sticker; to attendance; to turnover; to productivity; and to features of the job situation. Groups known in advance to differ on certain aspects of motivation and morale were compared. The reliability of the questionnaire measures was studied primarily by administering essentially the same questionnaire twice to forty-nine employees at the electronics company.

IV. INTEREST IN WORK INNOVATION INDEX

The first characteristic of people at work which we wished to assess is interest in work innovation. From an organizational point of view, much benefit can come from a search by employees at all levels for better ways to do things. For the individual, a continuing interest in innovation may represent an alertness which permits him to use well his mind and his abilities. For employees, interest in innovation may be also an indicator of general interest and involvement in their job.

Questionnaire Items

The following items appear to be the best indicators[1] of interest in innovation:[2]

1. In your kind of work, if a person tries to change his usual way of doing things, how does it generally turn out?

    (1)____ Usually turns out worse; the tried and true methods work best in my work
    (3)____ Usually doesn't make much difference
    (5)____ Usually turns out better; our methods need improvement

2. Some people prefer doing a job in pretty much the same way because this way they can count on always doing a good job.
    Others like to go out of their way in order to think up new ways of doing things. How is it with you on your job?

    (1)____ I always prefer doing things pretty much in the same way
    (2)____ I mostly prefer doing things pretty much in the same way
    (4)____ I mostly prefer doing things in new and different ways
    (5)____ I always prefer doing things in new and different ways

3. How often do you try out, on your own, a better or faster way of doing something on the job?

    (5)____ Once a week or more often
    (4)____ Two or three times a month
    (3)____ About once a month
    (2)____ Every few months
    (1)____ Rarely or never

---

[1] Three items used in a pre-test at TVA were dropped because of poor spread of responses and/or poor correlation with supervisors' rankings.

[2] Numbers in parentheses preceding each response category indicate the score assigned to each response.

4. How often do you get chances to try out your own ideas on your job, either before or after checking with your supervisor?

    (5)____ Several times a week or more
    (4)____ About once a week
    (3)____ Several times a month
    (2)____ About once a month
    (1)____ Less than once a month

5. In my kind of job, it's usually better to let your supervisor worry about new or better ways of doing things.

    (1)____ Strongly agree
    (2)____ Mostly agree
    (4)____ Mostly disagree
    (5)____ Strongly disagree

6. How many times in the past year have you suggested to your supervisor a different or better way of doing something on the job?

    (1)____ Never had occasion to do this during the past year
    (2)____ Once or twice
    (3)____ About three times
    (4)____ About five times
    (5)____ Six to ten times
    (6)____ More than ten times had occasion to do this during the past year.

An Index of Interest in Work Innovation (Index A) was computed by averaging the scores obtained on each of these six items. A shorter index (Index B) based on the three best items (Questions 1, 5, and 6) was also computed for TVA employees.[3]

Reliability

The test-retest reliability of the individual questions and of the six item index is presented in Table 1. These data were obtained at the electronics company.

Correlation Among Items

The correlation coefficients among the six items selected for measuring interest in innovation are presented in Table 2.

These data indicate moderate inter-correlations among most of the items, especially at the electronics company. Item 1, and to some extent Item 2, show poorer correlations with other items. It will be noted that whereas most of the questions concern fairly directly the employee's

---

[3] Index B has a median correlation of .84 (range of .65 to .88) with Index A at five TVA sites.

TABLE 1
Test-Retest Reliability of Measures of Interest in Work Innovation at Electronics Company (Product-Moment Correlation Coefficients, r)

	r	N
A. For Individuals		
Q1	.72	49
Q2	.72	49
Q3	.64	47
Q4	.67	48
Q5	.54	48
Q6	.85	48
Index (6 items)	.87	46
B. For Groups		
Index [a]	.92	13

[a] The data on the reliability of group scores was based on an index using questions 2 through 6.

behavior on the job, Item 1 refers to a more general felt need for improvement on the job. Item 1 relates more strongly to the recorded action of submitting suggestions at TVA, but less strongly to supervisors' rankings than do other items of the index.

Relation to Supervisors' Rankings

In discussion, supervisors were able to think of specific instances where employees in their units had suggested new or better ways of doing the job. They then ranked employees they personally knew on "looking out for new ideas."

At the time that judges ranked employees they knew on this characteristic, the following definition of "looking out for new ideas" was before them:

"Some people seem to be most on the lookout for new ideas — people who get a kick out of thinking up a different way of doing something. (It does not matter whether or not they try hard to do well at their regular job. Maybe they would rather take time to think of a new way to do something than to pitch in and get the job done the way it's supposed to be done.) The people who are most on the lookout for new ideas belong in *pile 1*.

"Some other people are less on the lookout for new ideas; they like to do things in the same way they have always done, and prefer the 'tried and true' methods. (They might be extremely hard-working, but simply less on the lookout for new ways of doing things.) These people belong in your *last pile*.

TABLE 2

Correlations Among Items Composing Interest in Work Innovation Index
(Product-Moment Correlation Coefficients)

A. At TVA (N = 834)

	Q2	Q3	Q4	Q5	Q6
Q1	.20	.08	.07	.10	.14
Q2		.16	.05	.15	.12
Q3			.41	.16	.36
Q4				.24	.34
Q5					.24

B. At Electronics Company (N = 223)

	Q2	Q3	Q4	Q5	Q6
Q1	.35	.10	.22	.20	.16
Q2		.31	.42	.38	.38
Q3			.45	.18	.26
Q4				.47	.56
Q5					.51

Table 3 shows the correlations between responses on questionnaire items and judges' rankings. These data show definite associations between scores on the Interest in Work Innovation Index and supervisors' rankings. Correlations are positive in fifteen of sixteen units and six of these are statistically significant. The magnitude of the positive correlation ranges from .04 to .69 with the median correlation being about .35 both at TVA and at the electronics company.[4] At TVA the association is greatest for those units within which there is most variation in interest in innovation — as indicated by standard deviation on the index and supervisors' ranking measures.[5] These units turn out to be the four engineering branches. The units in which there are the smallest correlations between questionnaire indices and supervisors' rankings are operator groups at the steam plants, while craftsmen groups at the steam plants are intermediate. These differences appear

---

[4] The short three-item Interest in Innovation Index B is related almost as strongly to supervisors' rankings as is the longer Index A.
[5] Data on variation is not presented here.

TABLE 3

Relation Between Scores on Index of Interest in Innovation (Index A) And Scores Based on Supervisors' Rankings of Extent to Which Employees are "Looking Out For New Ideas."[a] (Product-Moment Correlation Coefficient, r)

TVA	r	(N)
Div. 1: Civil Engineering	.41*	(33)
Div. 1: Electrical Engineering	.53*	(32)
Div. 2: Electrical Engineering	.34+	(29)
Div. 2: Civil Engineering	.54**	(24)
Steam Plant 1: Operating	.04	(42)
Steam Plant 2: Operating	.17	(42)
Steam Plant 3: Operating	.22	(48)
Steam Plant 1: Craftsmen	.45**	(47)
Steam Plant 2: Craftsmen	.33*	(43)
Steam Plant 3: Craftsmen	.20	(60)
Median	.34	(37)
Electronics Company		
Finance	.69*	(10)
Div. 1: Sales	.35	(13)
Div. 2: Production	.15	(13)
Div. 1: Engineering	-.02	(19)
Div. 2: Engineering	.51	(11)
Div. 3: Engineering	.34	(10)
Median	.35	(12)

*$p<.05$, two-tailed test.
**$p<.01$, two tailed test.
+$p<.05$, one-tailed test.

[a] See Methods section and Appendices A and B for description of procedures by which supervisors ranked employees.

related to the fact that operators' jobs are relatively standardized, thus permitting little innovation, while design engineers and, to some extent, craftsmen have far more leeway to try new ways of doing things.

At the electronics company, the highest correlation between the questionnaire index and supervisors' rankings is found within the finance unit. There are near zero correlations in a production unit (highly standardized work) and in one engineering unit. Moderate correlations are found in two other engineering units and in a sales unit.

As at TVA, correlations tend to be greater within those units where variation in index scores and in judges' rankings are greatest.[6]

Another way of looking at these data is to compare the index scores of all employees ranked low on "looking out for new ideas" by supervisors with the scores of those who were ranked medium and high on this quality. This involves some non-comparability in judges' rankings since each employee was judged in comparison only to those in his own unit. Such a "pooling" across units thus probably underestimates the actual relationship between index scores and rankings. However, it permits us to get a rough overall estimate of the magnitude of difference in index scores between those ranked differently by supervisors. Table 4 shows, separately for TVA and for the electronics company, mean scores on the interest in innovation index for those ranked high, medium, and low on this quality by supervisors. At TVA, there are highly significant differences among those ranked differently by supervisors. There is an average difference of almost four index points (on a scale ranging from 6 to 31) between those ranked high and those ranked low in "looking out for new ideas." At the electronics company, differences in mean scores are smaller but in the same expected direction.

Relation to Suggestions

TVA makes a serious effort to encourage its employees to make suggestions for changes aimed at increasing efficiency, safety, or the personal welfare of its employees.[7] In the organizational units covered in this study, one channel for such suggestions is the cooperative conference or committee of the particular unit. Suggested improvements are investigated by a committee (which includes the suggestor in some units) and are then discussed at the cooperative meetings by employee and management representatives. No cash prizes are given for cost-cutting suggestions. However, suggestions are recorded as favorable items on work records and outstanding suggestions get publicized in TVA publications.

New ideas also can be suggested or implemented through other channels than the suggestion system. Thus, the number of suggestions made through this channel is an imperfect measure of interest in innovation. However, people who do make suggestions through the cooperative program should, in general, be more interested in innovation than those who do not. Therefore, it would be expected that "suggestors," as a group, should score higher than others on the Index of Interest in Work Innovation.

---

[6] At TVA, Interest in Innovation scores correlate more strongly with supervisors' rankings of "looking out for new ideas" than with supervisors' rankings of other characteristics. This is true at the electronics company too, with the exception of supervisors' rankings of willingness to disagree; there Innovation scores correlate about equally with rankings of "looking out for new ideas" and rankings of willingness to disagree. These rankings are strongly correlated (See Appendix D).

[7] Although the electronics company has a suggestion system, it was not being vigorously encouraged at the time of the study. The number of suggestions was deemed too small to merit use in analysis.

TABLE 4

Mean Index Scores[a] on Interest in Work Innovation for Employees Ranked High, Medium, and Low by Supervisors

TVA	Score Based on Supervisors' Rankings[b]			
	Low (Up to 34th Percentile)	Medium (35th-65th Percentile)	High (66th Percentile or Higher)	Significance of Differences
Mean Index score	16.1	18.3	20.0	F=20.1
(N)	(116)	(176)	(102)	p<.001
Electronics Company				
Mean Index score	21.6	23.5	24.1	F=NS
(N)	(27)	(22)	(35)	High vs. Low p<.05 (2-tailed)

[a] Mean scores are adjusted to show the sum of scores for all items.
[b] See Chapter on Methods and Appendices A and B for description of supervisory ranking procedures.

Data from Records: For purposes of this study, data on suggestions were obtained from the minutes of the monthly meetings of the cooperative committees and conferences, covering the period from May, 1961, through April, 1962 — i.e., the year immediately prior to the questionnaire administration. In the units covered by this study, most of the suggestions made during this year fell in the category of improving efficiency. In examining the relation between the questionnaire index and suggestions made, we have combined all those who made one or more suggestions during the year covered into a single group. This is because of the relatively small size of this group in each site.

Table 5 shows the mean Interest in Work Innovation scores for suggestors and non-suggestors in the four TVA sites from which suggestion records were available. At the first site, an engineering division, only four persons were recorded as having submitted suggestions. However, the mean score for these men on the Interest In Innovation Index is so much higher than the mean score of other employees that the difference reaches statistical significance. At each of the three steam plants (where the suggestion program was stressed more than in engineering divisions) larger numbers of employees were recorded as having submitted suggestions. The mean interest in innovation score is higher for suggestors than for non-suggestors in each steam

TABLE 5

Mean Scores[a] on Interest in Work Innovation (Index A) for Those With and Without Recorded Suggestion at TVA[b] During the Year Preceding Questionnaire Administration

Unit	Suggestors Mean Index Score	(N)	Non-suggestors Mean	(N)	Significance of Difference
Engineering Div. 1	23.6	(4)	18.8	(193)	$p<.05$ (1-tail)
Steam Plant 1	17.4	(25)	17.0	(114)	p not signif.
Steam Plant 2	18.2	(52)	16.9	(74)	p not signif.
Steam Plant 3	20.0	(38)	17.6	(138)	$p<.01$ (2-tail)
All Steam Plants Combined	18.6	(115)	17.2	(326)	$p<.01$ (2 tail)

[a] Mean index scores are adjusted to show the sum of scores for all items.
[b] Data were taken from minutes of cooperative committees and conferences for the months of May 1961 through April 1962.

plant but the difference is statistically significant only for Steam Plant 3 and for all steam plants combined.[8]

Suggestions Reported by Respondents: The data presented in the previous section concern written records of suggestions to cooperative conferences or committees. In addition to this source of data, we asked respondents, "How many suggestions have you submitted to the cooperative conference or committee during the past three years?" Note that the period of time asked about in this question — three years — is longer than the period of one year for which written records were examined.

Table 6 shows the relation between scores on the interest in innovation index and the number of suggestions reported by TVA employees in five different locations, two engineering divisions and three steam plants. In all five locations, there are statistically significant though modest correlations (median $r = .29$) between index scores and reported number of suggestions.[9]

---

[8] For three steam plants combined, suggestors also score higher on the short three item index of interest in innovation (Index B) than do non-suggestors. The difference is significant at the .10 level, using a one-tail t-test. Of the individual items, question 1 is by far the most successful in distinguishing suggestors from non-suggestors.)

[9] For all TVA employees combined, the Interest in Innovation Index (Index B) has higher correlations with number of suggestions reported and recorded than do the indices of job motivation, identification with TVA, and acceptance of change. The Willingness to

TABLE 6

Relation Between Scores on Interest in Work Innovation Index[a] and Number of Suggestions Reported by TVA Employees for a Three-Year Period Preceding Questionnaire Administration (Product-Moment Correlation Coefficient, r)

Unit	r	(N)
Engineering Division 1	.29**	(192)
Engineering Division 2	.30**	(174)
Steam Plant 1	.19*	(134)
Steam Plant 2	.28**	(119)
Steam Plant 3	.34**	(170)
Median	.29	(170)

*$p<.05$, 2-tailed t-test.
**$p<.01$, 2-tailed t-test.

[a] Data are for the shorter three-item Index B.

Relation to Other Variables: It is of interest, in part to assess its "construct validity,"[10] to examine the relation of the measure of Interest in Work Innovation to other job-related variables. Group means on an Interest in Work Innovation Index[11] were computed for ninety work groups at TVA[12] and were correlated with group scores on variables which were expected to relate to interest in innovation. Table 7 shows these correlations, along with correlations of Interest in Innovation Scores with other measures of morale and motivation presented in this report.

These data show a moderate association between interest in innovation and a) an index of the difficulty of the job (e.g., how often "tough problems" come up); and b) an index of identification with one's occupation (e.g., expressed willingness to choose the same occupation again). There are smaller positive correlations between interest in innovation scores and indices of control over the means of doing the job, perceived opportunities for achievement, and feedback on job performance. The interest in innovation index shows close-to-zero correlations with indices of control over goals in work, need for achievement, and pressure from peers to do a good job.

Disagree with Supervisors Index has correlations with number of suggestions about equal to that of the Innovation Index.)

[10] See p. 12 for a brief discussion of construct validity.

[11] The shorter index, Index B, was used in this instance.

[12] Variance among ninety work groups on the Interest in Innovation Index B is slightly greater than variance within groups ($F = 1.28$).

TABLE 7

Relation of Scores on Interest in Work Innovation Index[a] to Scores on Other Job-Related Variables,[b] for 90 Work Groups at TVA
(Pearson Product-Moment Correlation Coefficient, r)

Variable Name

1. Job Difficulty .44**
2. Identification with own occupation .39**
3. Control over Work Methods .29**
4. Perceived Opportunity for Achievement .28**
5. Feedback on Performance .19
6. Control Over Goals in Work .13
7. Need for Achievement[c] .06
8. Pressure from Peers to do a good job -.05
9. General Job Motivation .36**
10. Willingness to Disagree with Supervisors .36**
11. Acceptance of Changes in Work Situation .12
12. Identification with TVA .00
13. Overall Satisfaction (with pay, promotion, supervisors, and peers) .21*

*$p<.05$, 2-tailed t-test.
**$p<.01$, 2-tailed t-test.

[a] The shorter three-item Index B was used for these correlations.
[b] Variables listed are all indices; each index is composed of several specific questions.
[c] This is the Achievement Risk Preference Scale developed by P. O'Conner and J. W. Atkinson (1960).

With respect to other measures of motivation and morale, the interest in innovation index shows a moderate association with an index of willingness to disagree with supervisors and with an index of general job motivation. It has only a small association with an index of overall job satisfaction and close-to-zero relationships with indices of acceptance of change and identification with TVA. (See later sections of the report for a description of measures of job motivation, willingness to disagree, acceptance of change, and identification with the work organization.)

Summary and Conclusions

Six questions were selected on the basis of reliability and validity evidence as indicators of employees' interest in innovation. The correlations among these items are positive but low at TVA and somewhat higher at the electronics company. The test-retest reliability of an

Index of Interest in Work Innovation, based on the six items, is .87 for individuals and .92 for groups, at the electronics company.

Each employee's score on the Interest in Innovation Index was compared to supervisors' rankings of this employee with respect to his "looking out for new ideas." The median correlation between index scores and supervisory rankings was .34 at TVA and .35 at the electronics company. Correlations with supervisors' rankings are higher in those units which have greatest variability in measures of interest in innovation. Mean index scores for all employees ranked low by supervisors differ substantially from the mean index scores of employees ranked medium or high by supervisors.

At TVA, one channel (though not the only one) through which interest in innovation can be demonstrated is the submission of formal written suggestions through a "cooperative program." Records were scanned for data concerning formal suggestions during the year preceding the questionnaire administration. Employees who made any suggestions during this period were compared to those who did not make suggestions, with respect to their scores on the Interest in Work Innovation Index. For all steam plants (where most suggestions are made) taken together, the index scores of the suggestors were significantly higher than those of the non-suggestors.

Index scores on the Interest in Innovation Index were also correlated with the number of formal suggestions which TVA employees reported making during the three year period preceding questionnaire administration. There are significant, though modest, correlations between index scores and number of suggestions reported in both engineering divisions and in all three steam plants.

Finally, scores on the Interest in Innovation Index were correlated with scores concerning aspects of the job situation and other relevant variables. Interest in innovation scores had strongest associations with indices of job difficulty, identification with one's own occupation, general job motivation, and willingness to disagree with supervisors.

In general, these data indicate that the Index of Interest in Work Innovation, while a rough one, shows adequate reliability and sufficient evidence of validity to warrant its use in making rough distinctions among groups of people (or among units). The potential user who has limited questionnaire space available should note the references to the short three item scale, which shows evidence of validity almost equal to the longer measure.

V. JOB MOTIVATION INDICES

It is evident that in most jobs, effective performance depends in part on positive motivation. Industrial psychologists and sociologists have therefore been much interested in employee motivation. Almost always such motivation has been inferred from other evidence — particularly productivity data — rather than directly measured. In some cases where production data are good and productive efficiency depends almost wholly on motivation, this kind of inference — rather than direct measurement — is quite acceptable. However, in most cases, the conditions that permit easy inference of motivation do not exist. Productive efficiency may be difficult to measure, or measured only for very large units, such as a whole plant. Technological differences and changes may make efficiency hard to compare among jobs and among units. Furthermore, efficiency may depend only in part — and in varying amounts — on motivation.

In such circumstances, it becomes useful to try to measure directly on the job.[1]

Questionnaire Items

From among a much larger set of items,[2] the following appear to have some degree of usefulness in assessing motivation on the job.[3]

1. On most days on your job, how often does time seem to drag for you?[4]

    (1)____ About half the day or more
    (2)____ About one-third of the day
    (3)____ About one-quarter of the day
    (4)____ About one-eighth of the day
    (5)____ Time never seems to drag

2. Some people are completely involved in their job — they are absorbed in it night and day. For other people, their job is simply one of several interests. How involved do you feel in your job?

---

[1] While interest in innovation may often be an indicator of job motivation, we are concerned here with job motivation from a more general standpoint, usually shown by general devotion of energy to job tasks.

[2] A total of 22 questionnaire items were tried at various times. Most were dropped either because they elicited little variation in responses or because they showed little or no correlation with validating evidence.

[3] Numbers in parentheses indicate the score assigned to each response.

[4] With regard to this question, it is interesting to note the following comment by Blauner: "Lack of involvement results in a heightened time-consciousness. If it were possible to measure "clock-watching," this would be one of the best objective indicators of this mode of alienation." (Blauner, 1964, p. 28.)

(1) ___ Very little involved; my other interests are more absorbing
(2) ___ Slightly involved
(3) ___ Moderately involved; my job and my other interests are equally absorbing to me
(4) ___ Strongly involved
(5) ___ Very strongly involved; my work is the most absorbing interest in my life.

3. How often do you do some extra work for your job which isn't really required of you?

(5) ___ Almost every day
(4) ___ Several times a week
(3) ___ About once a week
(2) ___ Once every few weeks
(1) ___ About once a month or less

(This question was used in the electronics company and in the appliance company, but not at TVA)

4. Would you say you work harder, less hard, or about the same as other people doing your type of work at (name of organization)?

(5) ___ Much harder than most others
(4) ___ A little harder than most others
(3) ___ About the same as most others
(2) ___ A little less hard than most others
(1) ___ Much less hard than most others

(This question was used in the electronics company and in the appliance company, but not at TVA)

Index scores based on the two questions asked at TVA (Index A) were computed for TVA employees. Index scores based on answers to the four questions (Index B) were computed for employees at the electronics company.

Reliability

Test-retest reliability coefficients are available at the Electronics Company for two of the items and for Index A which is based on these two items. These data are shown in Table 8.

Correlation Among Items

The correlation coefficients among items selected to measure job motivation are shown in Table 9.

Though these correlations are all positive, their small size (median) suggests that the single questions may be tapping somewhat different aspects of work motivation.

TABLE 8

Test-Retest Reliability for Two Job Motivation Items and for Job Motivation Index A, at Electronics Company (Pearson Product-Moment Correlation Coefficient, r)

Individual Scores	r	N
Q1	.80	47
Q2	.74	48
Q3	No reliability data; Q asked only once.	
Q4	No reliability data; Q asked only once.	
Index A (Items 1 and 2)	.80	46
Group Scores		
Index A (Items 1 and 2)	.83	13

Relation to Supervisors' Rankings

Supervisors chosen as judges were asked to discuss what "doing a good job" means concretely in their own units. They then ranked individual employees they knew on "concern for doing a good job" with the following definition before them:

"Some people *try especially hard* to do a good job on their regular assignment — they are highly conscientious or hard-working; always on

TABLE 9

Correlations Among Items Used in Indices of Job Motivation (Pearson Product-Moment Correlation Coefficient, r)

TVA (N = 834)

	Item 1
Item 2	.32

Electronics Company (N = 223)

	Item 2	Item 3	Item 4
Item 1	.38	.05	.17
Item 2		.22	.30
Item 3			.24

their toes; strongly concerned with doing just as good a job as they possibly can. (It does not matter whether or not they have new ideas about different ways of doing things, or whether they could take on a more difficult job.)

"Other people are *not quite so concerned* with doing a good job on their regular assignment. Maybe they aren't quite so conscientious; or sometimes they are less careful, or don't strain too much to finish a job on time. They may be good workers, or have new ideas, but you wouldn't consider them 'tops' in concern for doing a good job."

The rankings given by supervisors to each employee were converted into a percentile score showing each employee's relative position as judged by supervisors. (See Methods section and Appendices A and B for a description of the procedure of supervisory ranking and of scoring these data.) The ranking scores were then correlated with the scores employees received on the questionnaire index of job motivation.

At TVA, where the two item Index A is available, the correlations were generally low, with a median r of .15 for 10 units.[5] The low correlations appear to reflect in part a narrow range of variation within each unit both in index scores and in supervisory rankings of concern. For those two units (one electrical engineering branch and the operating section of one power plant) which were above the median in variation, both in index scores and in supervisory ranking scores, the correlations between index scores and ranking scores were higher, .27 and .47 respectively.[6]

In the electronics company, data on the full four-item Job Motivation Index B is available. Since correlations between scores on the four-item motivation index and ranking scores are available only in a few units, we have relaxed our usual requirement that data for ten or more persons in a unit be available in order to be presented. Table 10 shows the correlations between motivation index scores and supervisory ranking scores for six units of the electronics company.

The median correlation coefficient for the six units is .35. Five out of the six correlations are positive, two of these reaching statistical significance.[7] However, there is one sizable and statistically significant negative correlation in a production unit. This exception is difficult to explain. The measure of motivation does not seem inapplicable in production units since, as a later section will indicate, there was a

---

[5] In general, scores on Job Motivation Index A correlate more highly with supervisors' rankings of "Sense of Belonging to TVA" (median = .31) than with supervisors' rankings of "Concern for Doing a Good Job."

[6] No attempt was made in this study to pick units within which there was a wide range of motivation. In fact, many supervisors emphasized the relative similarity of their employees in this respect.

[7] However, scores on Motivation Index B correlate about as well with supervisory rankings of other employee characteristics as with rankings of "concern for doing a good job." Supervisory rankings have high intercorrelations (see Appendix D).

TABLE 10

Relation Between Scores on Four-Item Index of Job Motivation (Index B) and Scores Derived from Supervisors' Rankings of "Concern for Doing a Good Job," in Electronics Company.[a] (Pearson Product-Moment Correlation Coefficient, r)

	r	(N)
Div. 1: Engineering	.29	19
Div. 2: Engineering	.55*	14
Div. 3: Engineering	.17	7
Div. 2: Production Division	-.68*	11
Div. 1: Sales	.40	15
Purchasing	.59	8
Median	.35	12

*$p < .05$, two-tailed t-test

[a] See Methods section and Appendices A and B for description of procedures by which supervisors' ranking scores were obtained.

marked association between motivation index scores and efficiency data in another similar production unit.[8]

Relation to Absence

TVA. Table 11 shows the relation between scores on Job Motivation Index[9] and absence. The data are presented separately for one engineering division,[10] for steam plant operating personnel, and for steam plant non-operating personnel, because the general level of absence differes among these groupings. The data show, for individuals, small but statistically significant negative correlations (higher index score, less absence) within the engineering division and among steam plant non-operating employees. There are somewhat larger, but still modes (-.28, -.30) negative correlations among steam plant operating employees.

---

[8] When employees in all units at the electronics company were pooled, and the job motivation index scores of those ranked high in concern by their own supervisors were compared to the scores of those ranked medium and low, no significant differences in index scores appeared. This appears to be due to the fact, discussed elsewhere in the section, that the level of job motivation differs greatly across units in the electronics company. Therefore, supervisors' rankings cannot meaningfully be pooled across units. At TVA, where the level of job motivation across units is more even, a similar "pooled" analysis yielded significant differences in the job motivation index scores.

[9] Question 1, concerning whether "time drags" predicts attendance at TVA about as well as the two-item, Job Motivation Index A).

[10] Attendance data could not be obtained from the second engineering division.

TABLE 11

Relation Between Scores on Job Motivation Index A and Absences[a] For Individuals and for Units at TVA. (Pearson Product-Moment Correlation Coefficients)

	Individuals			Units		
	Full Day Absences	Total Absences	(N)	Full Day Absences	Total Absences	N
Engineering Div. 1	-.15*	-.08	(179)	.03	.15	(34)
Steam Plants: Non-operating	-.15*	-.16*	(225)	-.43*	-.53**	(23)
Steam Plants: Operating	-.28**	-.30**	(152)	-.50	-.46	(6)

*$p<.05$, 2 tailed t-test.
**$p<.01$, 2 tailed t-test.

[a] Data is for instances of absence during the one year period immediately preceding questionnaire administration. An instance of full day absence was defined as a continuous period of one or more days. Total instances of absence include instances of part day absence.

For work units (employees having the same immediate supervisor) negative correlations are fairly strong (-.43, -.53) and statistically significant for steam plant non-operating units. Negative correlations of about the same magnitude are also found among steam plant operating units — although the small number of operating units involved prevents the correlations from reaching statistical significance.[11] For units within the engineering division, however, there is not negative relation between mean index scores and number of absences. It may be noted that there are only about half as many full-day absences within the engineering division as within the steam plants, although many more part-day absences at the engineering division. It may be that differences in job motivation are not so much reflected in attendance differences among the largely professional engineering employees as among the steam plant employees. It is also relevant to note that there is much more variation in mean number of absences among steam plant units ($F = 3.32$, $p<.001$) than among engineering division ($F = 1.47$). This greater variation in steam plant absence undoubtedly contributes

---

[11] Job Motivation Index A has stronger negative correlations with absence than do the measures of interest in innovation, identification with TVA, acceptance of change, willingness to disagree with supervisors, and overall job satisfaction.

to the stronger association between scores on the job motivation index and absence among steam plant units.

It is noteworthy also that the correlation between the job motivation index and attendance was considerably stronger for group data than for individual data — at least in the steam plants. This appears to be due to two factors: 1) There was, as mentioned above, much more variance in attendance *among* groups in steam plants than *within* groups. 2) There was also considerably more variance in scores on the Job Motivation Index among groups than within groups. For groups in all sites combined, the ratio of between-groups to within-groups variance (F) equals 1.42. Since the principal variance in scores both on the motivation index and on attendance is for groups, rather than for individuals, it becomes clearer why the correlation should be much higher for groups.

Electronics Company. Data on attendance at the electronics company was available only for three groups of female production workers and one small group of engineering personnel. There was, in general, no relation between scores on the motivation questions and attendance for the female production workers. These employees differ from TVA employees covered not only in sex but also in the facts that (a) many, if not most, are responsible for the care of their small children when these children become sick, and (b) none of their absences is paid. Under these circumstances, it is perhaps plausible to expect that absence would be less likely to reflect poor motivation.

In the electronics engineering groups, which is more similar to TVA personnel, there was a correlation for seventeen individuals of -.20 between score on Motivation Index B and absence (i.e., higher motivation, less absence).

Appliance Company. At the appliance company, scores on the job motivation index and on absence (as well as other performance criteria) were available only for groups. Since question 4 applies mainly to comparisons of individuals within the same work group, this question was omitted from the job motivation index, which was based, therefore, upon questions 1, 2, and 3.[12] Scores for forty groups on this three-item index of job motivation (Index C) were correlated with mean number of absences over a twenty-two week period, approximately half of which period was prior to questionnaire administration. Motivation index scores correlate .10 with number of unexcused absences, a nonsignificant relation but in a direction opposite to that expected. However, the correlation for the forty work groups between average motivation scores and number of excused absences was -.33 (i.e., the higher the average motivation score, the fewer the absences). This correlation is statistically significant at beyond the .05 level, using a two-tailed t-test. It may be noted that the great majority of the absences in this company are excused so that the -.33 correlation coeffi-

---

[12] Preliminary analysis indicated that group means on question 4 showed no significant association with mean group absence nor with group performance criteria.

cient reflects the relation of Job Motivation Index scores to most of the company absences.

Relation to Productive Efficiency

Electronics Company. Production data, for a limited number of women employees who took the questionnaire, are available in one production unit of the electronics company. Volume of production was judged against a standard set by time and motion study on which a great deal of effort and money has been spent. Data on production volume is for an eight-week period preceding the questionnaire.[13] Data on the number of errors made by each individual, as a percentage of the average number of errors made by people doing that type of job, are also available in this unit. These latter data are for a period of twenty weeks preceding the questionnaire administration.

The correlation between individual scores on Job Motivation Index B and production volume was .54, for ten women production employees. This coefficient is statistically significant at the .05 level (one-tailed t-test). The correlation between job motivation index scores and number of errors made, for fourteen women production workers was -.30 (higher motivation, fewer errors), a relation in the expected direction but not statistically significant.[14] Scatter plots between the questionnaire index of motivation and errors made show that much of the association is accounted for by one person who made an unusual number of errors and scored very low on the index. However, the scatter plots between questionnaire index scores and production volume show a general association between these two variables.

Appliance Company. In the appliance company, higher level supervisors rated each of the work groups in their department on various aspects of efficiency. Ratings were made on a four point scale, ranging from excellent to poor. The ratings were repeated each week for a period of twenty-two weeks. (The questionnaire was administered at about the mid-point of this period.) At the end of the rating period, ratings were averaged for the entire period.

Ratings were made by supervisors on several cost factors, the extent to which work groups meet their schedules, and the quality of work. It may be noted that these criteria are incompatible to some extent since all-out effort to meet production schedules may sometimes result in extra costs or reduced quality. Moreover, a group's performance on these criteria is influenced by factors other than the motivation of group members. These other factors include the quality of incoming materials, excellence of supervisory administrative decisions, and machine quality. However, some association between motivation index scores and efficiency data would be expected.

---

[13] Production volume was computed each week for each employee. Figures here are an average of the weekly figures over an eight-week period ending two weeks prior to the questionnaire administration.

[14] Items 3 and 4 contribute most to the association between index scores and the two criteria of productive efficiency.

TABLE 12

Relation Between Mean Scores on Job Motivation Index C and Measures of Efficiency and Other Criteria[a] For Forty Work Groups at Appliance Company
(Pearson Product-Moment Correlation Coefficient, r)

	r
Productive Efficiency	
1. Costs (Mgmt. Ratings)	
Maintenance	-.26[+]
Supplies	-.28*
Scrap	-.20
2. Meeting Schedules (Mgmt. Ratings)	-.02
3. Quality (Mgmt. Ratings)	.17
Grievances (Records)	-.26[+]
Work Accidents (Records)	-.27[+]
No. Suggestions Installed (Records)	.46**
No. Suggestions Submitted (Records)	.23

*$p<.05$, two-tailed t-test.
**$p<.01$, two-tailed t-test.
[+]$p<.05$, one-tailed t-test.

[a] Data from company records are for the same twenty-two week period as that covered by the supervisors' ratings of productive efficiency.

The first part of Table 12 shows the relation between scores on the Job Motivation Index and supervisor ratings of aspects of production efficiency.[15] There are correlations in the expected negative direction (higher motivation, lower costs) between index scores and ratings of three types of costs; maintenance, supplied, and scrap. These correlations are low (in the .20's) but reach statistical significance. There is no association between job motivation index scores and ratings of how well units meet schedules. There is a small non-significant correlation in the expected direction between index scores and work quality.

Data on certain other criteria — including number of grievances, number of work accidents, number of suggestions submitted, and number of suggestions installed — were also available from records at the appliance company. As with ratings of efficiency, such occurrences as submitting a grievance or submitting a suggestion may be influenced by many factors other than motivation to do a good job. However, it is

---

[15] As with the data from the appliance company reported above, question 4, which is relevant primarily to the comparison of individuals within groups, was omitted from the index used for computing group scores.

interesting to see what association there is between the questionnaire index of motivation and these kinds of work behavior. The bottom part of Table 12 shows these correlations. There are associations in the expected direction between Job Motivation Index scores and number of grievances, number of accidents, and number of suggestions installed and number of suggestions submitted. Though most of these correlations are small, all but the last named are statistically significant.

Comparison of Occupational Groups

While "job motivation" items were at first chosen primarily for their ability to discriminate persons within groups, it would be expected that various occupational groups will differ on measures of work motivation. At the electronics company, there is an impressionistic contrast between production workers, on the one hand, and engineers and salesmen, on the other hand.

Production workers are primarily women who are doing tedious, though demanding, work in order to earn extra family income. Though their motivation to work efficiently enough to keep their job may be generally strong, the kind of positive motivation stemming from desire for achievement and commitment to one's occupation would be expected to be low in this group. Those in the engineering group would be expected to have more positive motivations, both because of commitment to their profession and because of the relative autonomy and challenge of their work. The salesmen group at the electronics company is a rather select one — made up of bright, well-educated men who have considerable responsibility; most of them have supervisory responsibility for more junior salesmen in addition to their own sales activities. They were expected to show up as high on the motivation questions — probably even higher than the engineering group.

Table 13 shows the responses to each of the four job motivation questions by each of the three occupational groups. On both Questions 1 and 2, there are sizable differences among the occupations, with salesmen giving the "high motivation" answers most often, engineering people next, and production workers least often. Question 3, concerning whether the employee does extra work, does not distinguish the engineering from the production group, although the salesmen again give the "high motivation" answers most often. Question 4, which asks whether the employee works harder than others "doing your type of work" is answered by the three occupations in the same order as Questions 1 and 2 — salesmen giving "high motivation" answers most often, engineering personnel slightly less often, and production workers least often. The differences among occupational groups in response to Question 4 are not as marked as the differences in response to Question 1 and 2. That clear differences do appear is especially noteworthy, however, in view of the fact that the question asks for comparisons to people in the same type of work.

TABLE 13

Responses to Job Motivation Questions By Persons In Different Occupational Groups at Electronics Company

Response Category	Salesmen (N=20)	Engineers and Allied Occupations* (N=106)	Production Workers (N=64)
Q1, How often time drags?			
About half the day or more	0%	0	14
About one-third	0	4	6
About one-quarter	0	10	17
About one-eighth of the day	5	30	27
Time never seems to drag	95	56	36
	100%	100%	100%
Q2, How involved in job?			
Very little involved	0	0	5
Slightly involved	0	5	8
Moderately involved	15	49	67
Strongly involved	55	40	11
Very strongly involved	30	6	9
	100%	100%	100%
Q3, Do extra work?			
About once a month or less	0	8	20
Once every few weeks	0	14	3
About once a week	10	20	18
Several times a week	30	39	20
Almost every day	60	19	39
	100%	100%	100%
Q4, Work harder than others?			
Much less hard	0	0	0
A little less hard	4	2	2
About the same	40	49	67
A little harder	35	44	20
Much harder	20	5	11
	100%	100%	100%

*This group is composed primarily of engineers, most of whom are electrical engineers. Draftsmen and technicians are also included.

Relation to Other Variables

We expected, on theoretical and common sense grounds, that job motivation would be related to a number of aspects of the job situation.

The existence or absence of such relations are relevant to the "construct validity"[16] of job motivation measures.

For ninety work groups at TVA, correlation coefficients are available showing the association between the Job Motivation Index A and other relevant variables. Table 14 shows these relations.

The first group of correlation coefficients shows the association of the job motivation measure to aspects of the job situation and of the individual to which it was expected to relate. Almost all of the correlations are positive and some reach a moderate size. The strongest association is between the Job Motivation Index and an index of perceived opportunities for achievement (r = .53). The latter index is composed of five questions which ask each employee how much chance he gets to try out his own ideas, to do the kind of things he's best at, to finish things, to use the skills he's learned for his present job, and to feel at the end of the day that he has accomplished something.

Group scores on the Job Motivation Index also show a marked association with an index of control over work methods (r = .43). The latter is based on fairly objective questions concerning such matters as the extent to which work methods are covered by rules. There are smaller but statistically significant associations with indices of identification with one's own occupation, feedback on performance, difficulty of work, and control over goals, as well as with perceptions that promotion depends on ability. The outstanding instance where an expect positive association failed to occur is between the job motivation index and a measure of personal need for achievement.

The second part of Table 14 shows the relation of the two-item job motivation index to several other criteria in which we have been interested. There is a marked negative association (r = -.56) with symptoms of psychological distress (nervousness, depression, chronic tiredness) on the job and a marked positive association (r = .50) with an index of overall satisfaction (based on questions concerning pay, promotion chances, the supervisor, and co-workers). The job motivation index has smaller positive correlations with measures of pride in work, identification with TVA, and interest in work innovation.

Summary and Conclusions

From among a much larger number of items tried as indicators of general job motivation, two questions (Q1 and 2) were selected at TVA as showing evidence of validity; these were combined into Index A. At the electronics company, two new items (Q3 and 4) showed evidence of validity and were added to the shorter index to form the four-item Index B. Those three items which are relevant for inter-group comparisons were combined into a third index, Index C, for use in computing group means at the appliance company.

Test-retest reliability data are available only for Index A, being .80 for individuals and .83 for small groups. Correlations among the four items used for the indices are positive but low.

---

[16] See p. 9 for brief discussion of construct validity.

TABLE 14

Relation Between Scores on Job Motivation Index A and Scores on Other Job-Related Variables, for 90 Work Groups at TVA. (Pearson Product-Moment Correlation Coefficient, r)

Variable Name	r With Job Motivation Index
Perceived opportunities for achievement index	.53**
Control over work methods index	.43**
Identification with own occupation index	.32**
Feedback on performance index	.29**
Difficulty of work index	.25*
Control over goals in work index	.24*
Extent to which promotion is perceived to depend on ability	.26*
Clarity of work goals index	.19+
Pressures from peers to do a good job index	.19+
Perceived opportunity for promotion	-.04
Need for Achievement Scale [a]	-.16
Symptoms of Psychological Distress index (nervousness, depression, tiredness)	-.56**
Overall Satisfaction (with pay, promotion, supervisor, and peers) index	.50**
Pride in work index	.38**
Identification with TVA	.33**
Interest in Innovation	.36**

*$p<.01$, two-tailed t-test.
**$p<.05$, two-tailed t-test.
+$p<.05$, one-tailed t-test.

[a] Achievement Risk Preference Scale (O'Connor and Atkinson, 1960).

At TVA, Index A generally has only a slight correlation with supervisory rankings of each employee's "concern for doing a good job." At the electronics company, Index B generally has a more marked association with supervisors' ratings of "concern" (median r = .35).

The relation of average job motivation index scores to group absence rates is generally substantial — especially for TVA steam plants, where Index A was used, and also for the appliance company where Index C was used. Data on the relation of index scores to absence for individuals comes mainly from TVA. In several parts of that organization, there are significant negative associations between scores on Job Motivation Index A and number of absences, though the size of these associations is not as great for individuals as for groups. The stronger correlations between motivation index scores and attendance at the group level appear to reflect the greater variation both in attendance and in motivation scores which occurs among groups as compared to among individuals in our samples.

Evidence on the relation between motivation index scores and work efficiency is available for individuals in one unit of the electronics company and for groups at the appliance company. For a small number of individuals at the electronics company, scores on Job Motivation Index B correlate .54 with production volume. Average Motivation Index C scores for work units at the appliance company have small positive relations to supervisors' ratings of several aspects of cost efficiency; are slightly related to ratings of work quality; and are not correlated with ratings of efficiency in meeting schedules. Average motivation index scores for work units at the appliance company also have generally small but positive correlations in the expected direction with grievances, with work accidents, with number of suggestions submitted, and with number of suggestions installed.

A comparison of different occupational groups shows expected differences in the distribution of responses to questions making up the job motivation index. A group of high-level salesmen and a group of engineering personnel show much higher "more motivated" scores than do production workers.

Scores on Job Motivation Index A show, for groups, a number of theoretically predictable associations with aspects of the work situation. The strongest of these associations are with perceived opportunities for achievement on the job, with control over work methods, and with identification with one's own occupation.

In general, the data show that the indices of job motivation have fairly good ability to distinguish among individuals or groups when there is considerable variation in index scores and/or on the criteria being predicted. The indices show less ability to detect fine differences within units where job motivation is relatively homogeneous. The indices appear, therefore, to be of greater use in the former situation.

Of the three indices used, Index B is probably best for use in distinguishing among individuals in the same unit or same type of unit. Index C is probably best for use in characterizing groups. Finally, it should be noted that additional reliability evidence is needed for Indices B and C. Additional items for the indices may also be desirable.

VI. ACCEPTANCE OF JOB CHANGES INDEX

In an era of swift technological and administrative changes, the degree of employee acceptance versus resistance to change is of considerable importance to managers. From the standpoint of individual well-being, general resistance to change may also be important in that it may indicate that the person feels threatened by the change in some way. It seems desirable therefore to be able to assess the extent to which employees react favorably or unfavorably to changes in the job situation.

Questionnaire Items

The following questions were used to try to assess employee readiness to accept changes introduced into the work situation:[1]

Q1. Sometimes changes in the way a job is done are more trouble than they are worth because they create a lot of problems and confusion. How often do you feel that changes which have affected you and your job at (name of organization) have been like this?

    (1)____ 50% or more of the changes have been more trouble than they're worth
    (2)____ About 40% of the changes
    (3)____ About 25% of the changes
    (4)____ About 15% of the changes
    (5)____ Only 5% or fewer of the changes have been more trouble than they're worth

Q2. From time to time changes in policies, procedures, and equipment are introduced by the management. How often do these changes lead to better ways of doing things?

    (1)____ Changes of this kind never improve things
    (2)____ They seldom do
    (3)____ About half of the time they do
    (4)____ Most of the time they do
    (5)____ Changes of this kind are always an improvement

Q3. How well do the various people in the plant or offices who are affected by these changes accept them?

    (1)____ Very few of the people involved accept the changes
    (2)____ Less than half do

---

[1] Numbers in parentheses indicate the scores assigned to each answer.

ACCEPTANCE OF JOB CHANGES INDEX

    (3)____About half of them do
    (4)____Most of them do
    (5)____Practically all of the people involved accept the changes

Q4. In general, how do you *now* feel about changes during the past year that affected the way your job is done?

    (1)____Made things somewhat worse
    (2)____Not improved things at all
    (3)____Not improved things very much
    (4)____Improved things somewhat
    (5)____Been a big improvement
        ____There have been no changes in my job in the past year.

Q5. During the past year when changes were introduced that affected the way your job is done, how did you feel about them *at first*?

At first I thought the changes would:

    (1)____Make things somewhat worse
    (2)____Not improve things at all
    (3)____Not improve things very much
    (4)____Improve things somewhat
    (5)____Be a big improvement
        ____There have been no changes in my job in the past year.

Questions 4 and 5 were preceded in the questionnaire by the following question:

Within the past year, have there been any *changes* in the way your job is done — like in the equipment you work with, the work procedures, the job standards and requirements, the kind of records you have to keep, etc.? (Answer only for changes affecting you in your *present* job classification.)

There have been:

    (1)____No changes; my work is done exactly the way it was a year ago.
    (2)____One or two changes; but it is not too different.
    (3)____A few changes; it's a little different now.
    (4)____Quite a few changes; things are fairly different.
    (5)____Many changes; my work is almost completely different now from the way it was a year ago.

An Index of Acceptance of Job Changes was computed by summing the response scores for questions 1 through 5.

Reliability

The test-retest reliability coefficients for employees at the electronics company are shown in Table 15.

TABLE 15

Test-Retest Reliability for Single Items and For Index of Acceptance of Changes at Electronics Company
(Pearson Product-Moment Correlation Coefficient, r)

Individual Scores	r	(N)
Q1	.42	(48)
Q2	.54	(49)
Q3	.35	(49)
Q4	.55	(36)
Q5	.58	(35)
Index (Q1 through 5)	.76	(34)
Group Scores		
Index (Q1 through 5)	.80	(9)

The data show a reliability for the five-item index of .76 for individuals and .80 for small groups. Group scores were, in many cases, based on the responses of only two or three persons. Scores for larger groups would be expected to be more stable and thus even more reliable.

Correlation Among Items

The correlations among the items composing the Acceptance of Job Changes Index are shown in Table 16.

In general the correlations among the items are of modest magnitude, suggesting that the single items may be tapping somewhat different aspects of acceptance of change. The highest correlation is between the two questions which ask how the employee felt at first about specific changes affecting his job and about how he feels now about these same changes.

Relation to Supervisors' Rankings

Supervisors acting as judges were asked to think of changes made in their units in the past few years — such as new procedures to follow, different types of equipment, reorganization of units, and shifting of personnel. A discussion about how people in their units reacted to these changes was stimulated.

The judges were then asked to rank those employees they know personally on degree of acceptance of changes. This quality was defined as follows:

"Some people are very willing to go along with the changes management has made — people who perhaps enjoy trying out new procedures,

TABLE 16

Correlations Among Items Making Up the Acceptance
of Job Changes Index
(Pearson Product-Moment Coefficients)

A. <u>TVA</u> (N = 834)

Q	2	3	4	5
1	.22	.19	.27	.22
2		.30	.34	.30
3			.21	.10
4				.70

B. <u>Electronics Company</u> (N = 223)

Q	2	3	4	5
1	.40	.15	.39	.28
2		.16	.38	.19
3			.26	.28
4				.65

or working with different equipment, or working in a new branch, etc. (It does not matter how hard these people work at their regular job, or whether they like to think up new ideas, or want to take more responsibility, etc.) The people who are most willing to go along with management's changes belong in *pile 1*.

"Other people find it hard to go along with changes. Perhaps they have become used to doing things in a certain way, and it is hard for them to get used to doing things in a different way. [Some of them might work very hard, or might feel they are really part of (work organization) but they find it difficult to change their way of doing things]. These people belong in your *last pile*."

Scores representing judges' rankings of employees (see Appendix B) were correlated with the scores employees received on the index of acceptance of change. These data are shown in Table 17. The data show considerable variation at TVA in the degree of association between index scores and supervisory rankings, with a median correlation for ten units of .25. Nine of the ten correlations are in the expected positive direction and four of these are statistically significant.

At the electronics company both rankings and index scores for ten or more persons were available in only two units. Scores of acceptance of change correlated .80 with supervisors' rankings in the sales unit and .40 in an engineering unit (both statistically significant).[2]

As with the relation of other index scores to supervisors' rankings, the magnitude of the correlations found appears to depend in part on the magnitude of variation in the characteristic. At TVA, the group which shows the highest correlation (.51) is the only unit which is above the median in variation both for index scores and for supervisory ranking of acceptance of change.[3] At the electronics company, the sales unit in which the .80 correlation is found has by far the greatest variation among the units shown in Table 12, both in acceptance of change index scores and in supervisors' rankings of employees on this characteristic.

Another way of examining the relation between index scores and supervisors' rankings is to compare the mean acceptance of change scores of all those ranked low, medium, and high by supervisors. As noted above, this procedure tends to reduce the size of the relationship since supervisors' rankings in one unit are not strictly comparable to rankings of supervisors in other units. However, it is of some interest to get a rough idea of the magnitude of difference among those ranked high, medium and low by supervisors.

Table 18 shows mean scores on the Acceptance of Job Changes Index for employees ranked low, medium, and high on this characteristic by supervisors. At TVA there is a mean difference of over two points (on a 21-point index) between the extremes of those ranked high and those ranked low. The differences among the three differently ranked groups are highly significant statistically. At the electronics company, the mean difference between the extremes of those ranked high and low by supervisors is larger than at TVA, being almost four index points. Although the samples at the electronics company are small, the mean differences among those ranked high, medium, and low are statistically significant.

Relation to Other Variables[4]

We expected, on the basis of our theoretical expectations and of previous research (Coch and French, 1948) that acceptance of change in the work situation will be related to the degree of employee participation in work decisions — especially decisions concerning the changes themselves. At TVA we have found high correlations between employee participation in a program of labor-management consultation, which

---

[2] Scores on the Acceptance of Work Changes Index correlate more strongly with supervisors' rankings of acceptance of change than with supervisors' rankings of other characteristics, both at TVA and at the electronics company.

[3] Data on variation in scores are not shown here.

[4] Data reported in this section are based on a modified acceptance of change index which includes questions 1 through 4 (above) but omits question 5. Question 5 was the weakest item at TVA though not at the electronics company.

TABLE 17

Relation Between Scores on Index of Acceptance of Change and Scores Derived from Supervisors' Rankings of This Characteristic[a] (Pearson Product-Moment Correlation Coefficient, r)

TVA	r	N
Div. 1: Civil Engineering	-.17	(15)
Div. 1: Electrical Engineering	.25	(23)
Div. 2: Electrical Engineering	.10	(25)
Div. 2: Civil Engineering	.25	(20)
Steam Plant 1 - Operating	.15	(32)
Steam Plant 2 - Operating	.35*	(39)
Steam Plant 3 - Operating	.04	(45)
Steam Plant 1 - Craftsmen	.51**	(34)
Steam Plant 2 - Craftsmen	.30+	(34)
Steam Plant 3 - Craftsmen	.29*	(49)
Median	.25	(33)
Electronics Company		
Div. 1: Engineering	.40+	(19)
Div. 1: Sales	.80**	(11)
Median	.60	(15)

*$p<.05$, two-tailed test
**$p<.01$, two-tailed test
+$p<.05$, one-tailed test

[a] See Methods section and Appendices A and B for description of procedures by which supervisors' ranking scores were obtained.

focuses especially on work improvements, and scores on the Acceptance of Job Changes Index (Patchen, 1965). For example, for eight separate "cooperative" programs (each covering a branch or division) acceptance of change scores correlated .90 ($p<.01$) with percentage of employees who reported having served on a cooperative program committee. Similarly high correlations were also found between other aspects of the vigor of participatory programs (e.g., amount of information received about the program, perceived attention given to employee suggestions) and average acceptance of change scores.

Acceptance of change scores also had significant correlations in the expected direction with several measures of employee influence in the immediate work situation. For ninety work groups at TVA [5]

---
[5] Acceptance of change scores at TVA vary more among the ninety work groups than within the work groups ($F = 1.72$, $p < .05$).

TABLE 18

Mean Scores on Index of Acceptance of Job Changes for Employees Ranked Low, Medium and High on this Characteristic by Supervisors[a]

	Scores Based on Supervisors' Rankings		
	Low (up to 34th Percentile)	Medium (35th-65th Percentile)	High (66th Percentile or Higher)
TVA			
Mean Index Score	16.2	17.6	18.4
(N)	(76)	(149)	(91)
Electronics Company			
Mean Index Score	16.3	19.3	20.1
(N)	(12)	(19)	(25)
Significance of Differences:	TVA, $F = 7.8$, $p < .001$		
	Electronics Company, $F = 5.8$, $p < .01$		

[a] See Chapter on Methods and Appendices A and B for description of supervisory ranking procedures.

average acceptance of change scores correlate .38 ($p<.01$) with an index of employee control over goals and .26 ($p<.05$) with an index of employee control over means of doing the job. The control over goals index is based on seven items covering such matters as how much influence employees have over setting of time schedules and the extent to which employees have a say about which things they will work on next. The control over means index is based on four questions covering such matters as the extent to which work methods are covered by formal rules and the likelihood that the immediate supervisor will go along with subordinates' suggestions.

For ninety work groups at TVA, acceptance of change scores correlate .42 ($p<.01$) with an index score of identification with TVA. (See later section of this report for a description of this measure.) Such an association between acceptance of change and organizational identification was expected since both variables were expected to be related to employee participation in decision-making. For the ninety TVA groups, average acceptance of change scores correlate .23 ($p<.05$) with Job Motivation Index A and .12 with the Interest in Work Innovation Index. There is essentially a zero correlation (negative, in fact, for some analyses) between acceptance of change scores and average satisfaction with pay and promotion. This lack of association is welcome since one would not wish the acceptance of change measure to reflect simply a general mood of satisfaction or dissatisfaction.

Summary and Conclusions

Five questions were selected as indicators of employee acceptance of change within the work situation. Correlations among these are positive but fairly small. Test-retest reliability coefficients for a five-item index were .76 for individuals and .80 for small groups.

Scores on the Acceptance of Job Changes Index have positive correlations with supervisors' rankings of each employee's acceptance of change in nine out of ten units at TVA and in both of two units at the electronics company. Five of the nine positive correlations are statistically significant; their magnitude varies considerably and appears to be largest in those units which have greatest variation in acceptance of change. Comparison of the mean index scores of employees who were ranked high, medium, or low by supervisors shows marked and statistically significant differences, especially at the electronics company.

Scores on the Acceptance of Job Changes Index show strong correlations, for units, with certain aspects of the work situation to which acceptance of change might, theoretically, be expected to relate. In particular, acceptance of change scores are strongly related to employee participation in work decision-making at TVA. Acceptance of Change scores appear to be independent of general satisfaction.

Overall, the Index of Acceptance of Job Change, while a rough measure, appears to be a useful one.

VII. WILLINGNESS TO DISAGREE WITH SUPERVISORS INDEX

In recent years, considerable attention has been given by psychologists and sociologists to concepts of participation and democratic-style supervision in industry. One indication of the presence of such a supervisory atmosphere is the willingness and felt freedom of employees to speak their minds -- even when this entails disagreement with supervisors. This section presents data on a short measure of employee willingness to disagree.

Questionnaire Items

The following questions appear to be the best among those tried[1] for assessing willingness to disagree with supervisors.[2]

1. How free do you feel to disagree with your immediate supervisor to his face?

    (1)___ It's better not to disagree
    (2)___ I'd hesitate some before disagreeing
    (4)___ I'd hesitate only a little
    (5)___ I wouldn't hesitate at all to disagree to his face

2. How many times during the past year have you told one of your supervisors about some policy or procedure on the job which you didn't like?

    (1)___ Never during the past year
    (2)___ Once
    (3)___ Twice
    (4)___ Three times
    (5)___ About five times
    (6)___ Six to ten times
    (7)___ More than ten times

Question 2 was made into two questions at the electronics company. These are:

2A. How many times during the past year have you told one of your supervisors about some *company policy* which you didn't like? CHECK ONE:

    (1)___ Never during the past year
    (2)___ Once

---

[1] Several other questions were dropped because of poor validity evidence at various stages of the project.

[2] Numbers in parentheses indicate the scores assigned to each response.

WILLINGNESS TO DISAGREE WITH SUPERVISORS INDEX

    (3)____Twice
    (4)____Three times
    (5)____About five times
    (6)____Six to ten times
    (7)____More than ten times

2B. How many times during the past year have you told one of your supervisors about some *work procedure* which you didn't like? CHECK ONE:

    (1)____Never during the past year
    (2)____Once
    (3)____Twice
    (4)____Three times
    (5)____About five times
    (6)____Six to ten times
    (7)____More than ten times

3. When you don't like some policy or procedure on the job, how often do you tell your opinion to one of your supervisors?

    (1)____Very rarely or never
    (2)____About a tenth of the time
    (3)____About a quarter of the time
    (4)____About half of the time
    (5)____About three-quarters of the time
    (6)____Almost always

An index (Index A) based on the sum of scores on questions 1, 2, and 3 was computed for TVA employees. A parallel index (Index B) based on questions 1, 2A, 2B, and 3 was computed for employees at the electronics company.

Reliability

Test-retest reliability coefficients for employees at the electronics company are shown in Table 19.

Correlation Among Items

The correlation among items selected for measuring willingness to disagree with supervisors are shown in Table 20.

In general the weakest correlation is between item 1 and item 2 (or 2A and 2B). Item 1 appears to reflect a subjective feeling of freedom to speak out freely *whenever* one chooses to, but not necessarily often. Items 2, 2A and 2B appear to reflect more a frequency of expressing disagreement. Item 3 appears to be fairly closely associated with both of these aspects at TVA, but more with the subjective feeling of freedom at the electronics company.

TABLE 19

Test-retest Reliability for Index of Willingness to Disagree with Supervisors and for Items of this Index at Electronics Company (Pearson Product-Moment Correlation Coefficient, r)

Individual Scores	r	(N)
Q1	.74	(47)
Q2A	.77	(48)
Q2B	.49	(48)
Q3	.46	(47)
Index B (Q1, 2A, 2B, 3)	.74	(47)
Group Scores		
Index B (Q1, 2A, 2B, 3)	.78	(14)

Relation to Supervisors' Rankings

Supervisors were asked whether "it ever happens that a supervisor (such as a section, branch, or division head) makes a decision that people under him think is wrong?" They were encouraged to discuss examples of this kind and how disagreement was expressed. Supervisors were then asked to rank employees on willingness to disagree, with the following definition of this characteristic before them.

"Some people would be most willing to speak up frankly, and express their disagreement directly to their supervisor. (It does not matter, of course, whether these people are trying hard to do a good job, or whether they are on the lookout for new ways of doing things.) People who are most willing to express their disagreements belong in *pile 1*.

Other people would generally not speak out to the supervisor — they would rather accept the decision (or maybe gripe about it to their friends) instead of making a fuss about it. These people belong in your *last pile*."

It was emphasized to supervisors that what we were asking about was *not* how *often* a person disagrees but how ready he is to express those disagreements he has.

Table 21 shows the relation between scores on the questionnaire index of willingness to disagree and scores on this characteristic derived from supervisors' rankings. For ten TVA units, the correlation coefficients between index scores and supervisor ranking scores ranges from .02 to .67 with a median r of .34. All ten correlations are positive and seven are statistically significant. Correlation coefficients are

WILLINGNESS TO DISAGREE WITH SUPERVISORS INDEX

TABLE 20

Correlations Among Items Composing the Index of Willingness to Disagree with Supervisors (Pearson Product-Moment Coefficients)

TVA (N = 834)

Q	1	2	3
1		.27	.43
2			.45

Electronics Company (mean r for 9 units)

Q	2A	2B	3
1	.18	.07	.49
2A		.45	.23
2B			.17

generally higher in engineering units and in steam plant operating units than in steam plant crafts units. As has been found with other measures, the correlations tend to be larger in those units which have the greatest variation in scores, both on the index and on ranking scores.

For smaller samples in five units of the electronics company, correlations between index scores and supervisor ranking scores range from .23 to .54, with the median r being .39. Since the sample sizes are smaller in the electronics company, however, only one of the coefficients reaches statistical significance.[3]

Another way of examining the relation between scores on the willingness to disagree index and supervisor ranking scores is to compare the mean index scores of all employees ranked low on this characteristic by supervisors with those ranked medium or high. Table 21 presents these data. At TVA, mean scores on the Willingness to Disagree Index differ significantly among those ranked differently by supervisors. At the extremes, there is a greater than three index point difference (on a sixteen point scale) between the average index scores of those ranked low by supervisors and those ranked high in willingness to disagree. At the electronics company, where the range of index scores is twenty-three points,[4] a parallel but proportionately somewhat smaller

---

[3] Scores on the Willingness to Disagree Index correlate more strongly with supervisors' rankings of Willingness to Disagree than with supervisors' rankings of other characteristics, both at TVA and at the electronics company.

[4] Note that the index contains an additional question at the electronics company.

TABLE 21

Relation Between Scores on Index of Willingness to Disagree with Supervisors[a] and Employee Scores on this Characteristic Derived from Supervisors Rankings[b]
(Pearson Product-Moment Correlation Coefficient, r)

TVA	r	N
Div. 1: Civil Engineering	.48**	(31)
Div. 1: Electrical Engineering	.36[+]	(27)
Div. 2: Electrical Engineering	.67**	(30)
Div. 2: Civil Engineering	.20	(25)
Steam Plant 1: Operating	.36*	(41)
Steam Plant 2: Operating	.45**	(48)
Steam Plant 3: Operating	.31*	(54)
Steam Plant 1: Crafts	.02	(52)
Steam Plant 2: Crafts	.09	(42)
Steam Plant 3: Crafts	.28*	(60)
Median, TVA Units	.34	(42)
Electronics Company		
Div. 1: Engineering	.23	(17)
Div. 2: Engineering	.54[+]	(12)
Div. 2: Production	.24	(10)
Div. 1: Sales	.39	(11)
Finance	.44	(10)
Median, Electronics Company	.39	(11)

*$p<.05$, two-tailed test.
**$p<.01$, two-tailed test.
[+]$p<.05$, one-tailed test.

[a] Index A used at TVA; Index B at electronics company.
[b] See Methods section and Appendices A and B for procedures by which supervisory ranking scores were obtained.

difference is found among the mean index scores of those ranked high, medium, and low by supervisors. In the case of the electronics company, the difference among the three mean scores is not statistically significant but the difference between the two extreme groups (those ranked low and those ranked high) is significant.

Relation to Other Variables

We made no advance predictions about the association of other

TABLE 22

Mean Scores on Indices of Willingness to Disagree with Supervisors for Employees Ranked Low, Medium, and High on this Characteristic by Supervisors.

	Supervisors Ranking Score		
	Low (0-34th Percentile)	Medium (35th-65th Percentile)	High (66th Percentile or Higher)
TVA			
Mean Index Score (Index A)	10.1	12.1	13.2
(N)	(127)	(184)	(103)
Electronics Company			
Mean Index Score (Index B)	14.4	16.0	17.3
(N)	(28)	(20)	(30)

Significance of Differences: TVA, $F = 17.7$, $p < .001$

Electronics Company, $F = 2.8$, p = n.s.
High vs. Low: $t = 2.28$ $p < .05$ (two-tail)

variables on which we have data with willingness to express disagreement with supervisors. We therefore cannot assess the construct validity of this index. It is of interest, however, to note the degree of association of the Willingness to Disagree Index with some other variables. For ninety work groups at TVA,[5] scores on the Willingness to Disagree with Supervisors Index correlates .36 ($p < .01$) with scores on the Interest in Work Innovation Index. They have no noticable association with scores on measures of overall job satisfaction, of job motivation, of identification with TVA, or of acceptance of changes introduced by management.

The variable noted as most strongly related to willingness to express disagreement, at TVA, is control over goals in the work situation ($r = .42$, $p < .01$). Control over goals is measured by an index based on seven questions concerning the amount of say or influence the employee has (or whether he is consulted) about such matters as setting of time deadlines and establishing quality standards for the work. Of course other variables, such as freedom from arbitrary penalty by management (which we did not attempt to measure), may also be expected to relate to the willingness to voice one's opinion openly.

---

[5] There is considerable variance among the groups on the willingness to disagree index, but not more than within groups ($F = .95$).

Summary and Conclusions

Four questionnaire items were selected as showing some validity as indicators of employees' willingness to express disagreements they may feel with supervisors. Indices based on these questions differ somewhat between TVA and the electronics company since question 2 at TVA was made into two separate questions at the electronics company. The four-item Index B had a test-retest reliability of .74 for individuals and .78 for groups. The size of correlation among items varies and suggests that some items reflect more the felt freedom to speak out while other items represent more the actual frequency of expressing disagreement.

Scores on the indices of willingness to disagree were correlated with scores derived from supervisors' rankings of employees on this characteristic. At both TVA and the electronics company, correlations were all positive, of moderate size on the average, and often statistically significant. When the same data were examined from another perspective, there were found to be marked and statistically significant differences among the mean index scores of employees ranked high, medium and low by supervisors.

Group scores on the Willingness to Disagree with Supervisors Index A showed marked positive correlations with the Interest in Work Innovation Index and with an index of control over goals in the work situation. The willingness to disagree index is not appreciably correlated, either positively or negatively, with measures of job satisfaction, job motivation, or identification with the work organization.

Overall, the reliability and validity evidence indicates that the Willingness to Disagree with Supervisors Index may often be useful as a rough measure of this characteristic. The four item index is probably preferable to the three-item one, partly to provide another item for a short index and partly because questions 2A and 2B are more specific than question 2. While the validity evidence presented here focuses on individual variations in willingness to disagree, the measure will probably most often be useful for assessing differences among groups with different supervisors or different management "climates."

VIII. IDENTIFICATION WITH THE WORK ORGANIZATION INDICES

The subject of employee identification with the organization for which they work has been frequently discussed. But rarely has there been an attempt to measure employee identification.

We have defined organizational identification as meaning a sense of solidarity (i.e., of common interest and purpose) with other members of the organization, especially with the top leaders.[1] Such a sense of solidarity will usually be accompanied by a willingness to label oneself as an organization member and by a willingness to defend and support the organization.

Questionnaire Items

The following items appear to be the best among those tried[2] for assessing identification with the organization.[3]

1a. If you could begin working over again, but in the same occupation as you're in now, how likely would you be to choose TVA as a place to work?

    (1)___ Definitely would choose another place over TVA
    (2)___ Probably would choose another place over TVA
    (3)___ Wouldn't care much whether it was TVA or some other place
    (4)___ Probably would choose TVA over another place
    (5)___ Definitely would choose TVA over another place for my occupation

1b. An identical question was used at the private company except for the name of the organization.

2a. Following are two somewhat different statements about the relations between management and employees at TVA:

    A. The relations between management and employees at TVA are much different than in private industry, because in TVA both are working together toward the same goal of building the Valley.

    B. Relations between management and employees at TVA are not really very different than in private industry;

---

[1] This definition is consistent with the concept of identification used by Willerman (1949) and by Sherif and Cantril (1947).
[2] Five additional items were tried in various forms of the questionnaire but were dropped because of poor validity or reliability.
[3] Numbers in parentheses indicate the score assigned to each response category.

management is looking out for the organization's interests, and employees have to look out for their own interests.

Which of the two statements above comes closer to *your* own opinion?

(5)____Agree completely with A
(4)____Agree more with A than with B
(2)____Agree more with B than with A
(1)____Agree completely with B

The following almost identical question was used at the electronics company:

2b. Following are two somewhat different statements about the relations between management and employees at (name of company):

> A. The relations between management and employees at (company name) are much different than in most other companies, because in (company name) both are working together toward the same goals.
>
> B. Relations between management and employees at (company name) are not really very different than in other companies; management is looking out for the organization's interests, and employees have to look out for their own interests.

Which of the two statements above comes closer to *your* own opinion?

(5)____Agree completely with A
(4)____Agree more with A than with B
(2)____Agree more with B than with A
(1)____Agree completely with B

3a. How do you feel when you hear (or read about) someone criticizing the TVA method of public power or comparing it unfavorably to private power?

(1)____I mostly agree with the criticism
(2)____It doesn't bother me
(4)____It gets me a little mad
(5)____It gets me quite mad
____I never hear or read such criticism

3b. The following similar question was used at the electronics company:

How do you feel when you hear (or read about) someone criticizing (company name) or (company name) products, or comparing (company name) unfavorably to other companies?

IDENTIFICATION WITH THE WORK ORGANIZATION INDICES

    (2)___ It doesn't really bother me; I don't care much what other people think of (company name)
    (4)___ It bothers me a little
    (5)___ It bothers me quite a bit; I'm anxious to have people think well of (comapny name)
    ___ I never hear or read such criticism

4a. If someone asked you to describe yourself, and you could tell only one thing about yourself, which of the following answers would you be most likely to give? (Put a *number 1* next to that item.)

    ___ I come from (my home state)
    ___ I work for TVA
    ___ I am a (my occupation or type of work)
    ___ I am a (my church membership or preference)
    ___ I am a graduate of (my school)

If you could give two answers, which of the items above would you choose second? (Put a *number 2* next to that item.)

If you could give three answers, which one of the items would you choose third? (Put a *number 3* next to that item.)

(Scored 1 through 4, with those choosing TVA as first choice getting a 4 and those not choosing it at all getting a 1.)

4b. An identical question was used for the electronics company, except for the name of the organization.

5. If you have or were to have a son, how would you feel if someone suggested that he work for the same company that you work for? (If you are a woman, answer for a daughter.)

    (5)___ Would completely approve
    (4)___ Would generally approve, but with some reservations
    (3)___ Would neither approve nor disapprove
    (2)___ Would disapprove a little
    (1)___ Would strongly disapprove

6. In general, how often do you tell someone in your immediate family (wife, child, parent, brother, sister) about some project that TVA has done or is doing?

    (5)___ Once a week or more
    (4)___ Several times a month
    (3)___ About once a month
    (2)___ Once every few months
    (1)___ About once a year
    ___ Don't have any immediate family to talk to.

7. In general, how often do you tell someone *outside* your immediate family (friend, neighbor, store clerk, etc.) about some project that TVA has done or is doing?

(5)___ Once a week or more
(4)___ Several times a month
(3)___ About once a month
(2)___ About every few months
(1)___ About once a year

8. During the past two years, how many times has your part of TVA had a dinner or picnic or other social event outside of office hours?

(5)___ Five or more times
(4)___ Four times
(3)___ Three times
(2)___ Two times
(1)___ Once
(0)___ Never that I know of

IF ANY SOCIAL EVENTS HELD:

How many of these social events did you attend?

(5)___ Five or more
(4)___ Four
(3)___ Three
(2)___ Two
(1)___ One
(0)___ None

(Score on item 8 was proportion of events attended, re-coded on a five point scale.)

The first four items were asked at both TVA and at the electronics company. Item 5 was asked only at the electronics company and items 6 through 8 were asked only at TVA. Three main indices were computed on the basis of these questions: 1) Index B, based on the sum of scores on three items (Q1, 2 and 3) used both at TVA and at the electronics company; 2) Index C, which adds to Index B the question (Q5) used only at the electronics company; 3) Index D, a seven item index including all items used at TVA which showed evidence of validity.[4]

Reliability

Test-retest reliability coefficients for individual questions and for indices based on these questions are presented in Table 23. This table includes data which was available from one engineering division at TVA,[5] as well as for the electronics company. For individuals, the reliability of scores is .69 for Index B, .75 for Index C,[6] and .71 for

---

[4] Index B correlates .93 with Index C for all individual employees at the electronics company. Index B correlates .75 with Index D for all individual employees at TVA.

[5] While most of the questions used in other indices changed somewhat between pretest and final administration at TVA, most of the identification items remained the same.

[6] Question 4 was omitted from Index C because it pulls down the reliability of the index.

TABLE 23

Test-Retest Reliability of Items and Indices
Measuring Identification with the Work Organization
(Pearson Product-Moment Correlation Coefficients, r)

Individual Scores	Electronics Company		TVA	
	r	(N)	r	(N)
Q1	.60	(49)	.68	(32)
Q2	.61	(49)	not asked twice	
Q3[a]	.58	(48)	.71	(29)
Q4	.46	(45)	.35	(29)
Q5	.49	(48)	not asked	
Q6	not asked		.27	(31)
Q7	not asked		.61	(32)
Q8	not asked		.50	(32)
Index A (Q1 and 3)	-	-	.75	(29)
Index B (Q1, 2, 3)	.69	(48)	-	-
Index C (Q1, 2, 3, 5)	.75	(49)	-	-
Index D-2[b] (Q1, 3, 4, 5, 6, 7)	-	-	.71	(32)
Group Scores				
Index A (Q1 and 3)	-	-	.98	(5)
Index B (Q1, 2, 3)	.75	(13)	-	-
Index C (Q1, 2, 3, 5)	.79	(14)	-	-
Index D-2[b] (Q1, 3, 4, 5, 6, 7)	-	-	.99	(5)

[a] Response categories for this question at the second administration differed somewhat from response categories at the first administration.
[b] Index D-2 is the same as Index D, except that Q2 is omitted.

Index D-2.[7] Inspection of Table 23 shows that questions 4 and 6 have low reliability coefficients, which are undoubtedly pulling down the reliability of Index D-2. However, in view of the ability of these items to distinguish between people who show or do not show identification-related behavior at TVA, these items were retained in Identification Index D.

Group scores at the electronics company have a test-retest reliability of .75 for Index B and .79 for Index C. To estimate reliability of group scores at TVA, data on only five units are available. For

---

[7] Index D-2 has all the items of Index D except Q2, for which reliability data are not available.

TABLE 24

Correlations Among Items Used in Indices of Identification with Work Organization
(Pearson Product-Moment Coefficients)

TVA (N = 834)

Q	2	3	4	6	7	8
1	.24	.33	.22	.08	.07	-.06
2		.18	.20	.01	.05	.04
3			.19	.06	.03	.06
4				.04	.09	-.05
6					.60	.00
7						.06

Electronics Company (N = 223)

Q	2	3	4	5
1	.43	.36	.32	.43
2		.36	-.28	.25
3			-.15	.26
4				-.10

these units the test-retest correlation coefficients are almost perfect (.99). Though this figure is undoubtedly higher than should be usually expected, chance variations may be expected to be generally random within large units, thus giving greater stability of scores for units than for individuals.

Correlation Among Items

Table 24 shows the correlation among items used to make up indices of identification with the work organization.

At both TVA and at the electronics company items 1 through 4 (and also item 5 at the electronics company) tend to cluster together, even though the magnitude of correlation is not high. The median correlation for items 1 through 5 is .29 at the electronics company and is .21 for items 1 through 4 at TVA.

Items 6 through 8, however, show almost no intercorrelations among themselves (with the notable exception of similar items 6 and 7).

It is apparent that Index D, which includes items 1 through 7, is not measuring a single dimension of feeling toward the work organization. A disposition to tell people about TVA appears independent of the attitudes toward the organization expressed in questions 1 through 4 and both appear independent of attendance at TVA social events. Yet items of all types show an ability to distinguish people who display a TVA sticker on their car from those who don't and to distinguish those who resigned from TVA from those who did not. Thus, while recognizing that this set of items is not homogenous, it appears useful to use all of them to predict identification-related behavior.

Relation to Supervisors' Rankings

We asked supervisors whether some people in their units act more like they "really belong to TVA" (or to the electronics company) than do other employees. We asked this question with some doubt about the ability of supervisors to judge such an abstract characteristic, but supervisors were able to think of a number of specific indicators of a sense of belonging. At TVA, these include: being on the lookout for jobs outside TVA; accepting or not accepting extra pay for short periods of overtime; wasting of materials with the apparent attitude — "TVA has plenty of money;" saying "we" when talking about TVA; wearing TVA pins or using TVA car stickers; talking about whether a job is up to "TVA standards;" and expressed reaction to newspaper stories about TVA.

Specific behavioral indicators mentioned by supervisors at the electronics company were generally similar, along with such indicators as whether the individual "talks up" and buys company products and whether he is active in employee clubs and associations.[8]

TVA supervisors were asked to rank employees they know on their "sense of belonging to TVA" using the following description as a reminder:

"Some people seem most like 'old TVA'ers'— people who take special pride in the things TVA has done, and act as if they really belonged to TVA. (It does not matter whether they are on the lookout for new ideas, or want more responsibility, or whether they agree or disagree with the supervisor, etc.) The people who seem to show the strongest sense of belonging should go in *pile 1*.

Other people do not express a very strong sense of belonging to TVA. (They may be very hard-working, or on the lookout for new ideas, or willing to take responsibility, but they don't feel much like 'real TVA'ers.' These people should go in your *last pile*."

Supervisors at the electronics company had a similarly worded description before them.

---

[8] Only a small number of employees participated in such clubs and data identifying these was not collected.

62   EMPLOYEE MOTIVATION AND MORALE

Table 25 shows the correlations between questionnaire indices of identification with the work organization and supervisors rankings of employees' "sense of belonging" to the organization.

At TVA, there are positive correlations between Index B scores and supervisor rankings in eight out of ten units. Five of the eight positive correlations are statistically significant. The median correlation for all ten units is .24. Results using Index D show correlations which tend to be somewhat lower.[9]

At the electronics company, there are sufficient relevant data in only two units — one engineering and one sales. In both of these units there are positive correlations between identification index scores and supervisor rankings of "sense of belonging." The average correlation is .36 and the relation for one of the units is statistically significant.[10]

Relation to Displaying an Organizational Sticker

Perhaps the most direct available behavioral indicator of organizational identification which may be used to assess the validity of the identification measures is whether or not a TVA employee has a TVA sticker on his car.

Data on this subject were obtained from the following question:

"Have you ever had a TVA sticker on your car (aside from those required for parking)?"

____Yes, I have one on my car now
____Yes, I don't now, but I used to have one
____No, I never had one on my car
____Where I work you can't get TVA stickers
____I don't have a car

Figure 1 shows a very marked relation between scores on the index of organizational identification (Index D shown) and the likelihood of displaying a TVA sticker. Among those with the lowest identification scores, only 9 percent reported the present display of a TVA sticker while 85 percent said they did not show one now. As identification

---

[9] At TVA, the Identification with Organization Index correlates more strongly with supervisors' rankings of sense of belonging to the organization than with supervisors' ranking of other characteristics. At the electronics company, the same is true with the the exception that Identification scores correlate somewhat more strongly with rankings of acceptance of change than with rankings of sense of belonging to the organization. Rankings of these two qualities are strongly correlated (See Appendix D).

[10] The relation between scores on the indices of identification and supervisors' rankings of this characteristic were also examined by comparing the mean identification scores of all those ranked low, medium and high on "sense of belonging." At TVA, there are small but statistically significant differences in the expected direction among the mean index scores of those ranked high, medium, and low by supervisors. (This is true whether Index D or Index B is used). At the electronics company, there are also differences in the expected direction but these differences are smaller and are not statistically significant. As noted in previous sections, the procedure of pooling rankings across units tends to reduce the size of the relation between index scores and supervisors' rankings, since each employee was ranked relative to those in his own unit.

IDENTIFICATION WITH THE WORK ORGANIZATION INDICES

TABLE 25

Relation Between Scores on Questionnaire Indices of Identification With the Work Organization and Scores Based on Supervisors' Rankings of Employees' "Sense of Belonging" to the Organization[a]
(Pearson Product-Moment Correlation Coefficient, r)

	Index B		Index C		Index D	
	r	(N)	r	(N)	r	(N)
TVA						
Div. 1: Civil Engineering	.40*	(32)	-	-	.37*	(34)
Div. 1: Electrical Engineering	.34*	(32)	-	-	.25	(33)
Div. 2: Electrical Engineering	.13	(28)	-	-	.32+	(29)
Div. 2: Civil Engineering	.12	(21)	-	-	.06	(22)
Steam Plant 1: Operators	-.16	(40)	-	-	-.12	(40)
Steam Plant 2: Operators	.30*	(42)	-	-	.13	(42)
Steam Plant 3: Operators	.19	(49)	-	-	.01	(52)
Steam Plant 1: Mechanical	-.06	(38)	-	-	.15	(39)
Steam Plant 2: Mechanical	.39*	(37)	-	-	.19	(41)
Steam Plant 3: Mechanical	.28*	(55)	-	-	.32*	(59)
Median	.24	(37)			.17	(40)
Electronics Company						
Div. 1: Engineering	.40+	(22)	.43*	(22)	-	-
Div. 1: Sales	.31	(14)	.28	(14)	-	-
Median	.36	(18)	.36	(18)		

*p<.05, two-tailed test.
+p<.05, one-tailed test.

[a]See Methods section and Appendices A and B for procedures by which supervisory ranking scores were derived.

scores increase, the proportion displaying TVA auto stickers steadily increases also. Among those with the highest identification scores, 51 percent report now displaying a TVA sticker as opposed to 44 percent who do not. (The data using the shorter identification Index B, rather than Index D, are similar to the data shown, but the differences are less strong.[11]

One may raise the question, of course, as to why an even larger proportion of the "high identification" group do not have TVA stickers. The answer may be due in part to the fact that these stickers are not

---

[11] Among those lowest on Identification Index B, 9 percent report displaying a sticker. Among those highest on Identification Index B, 36 percent report displaying a sticker. These percentages are based on only those with an opportunity to display a sticker.

TABLE 26

Mean Scores on Index of Identification with Work Organization[a] for Electronics Company Employees with Different Lengths of Previous Employment and Different Expected Length of Future Employment.

	Mean Identification Score	(N)
Previous Service: Up to 3 years		
Expected future service:		
Up to 2 years	3.59	(11)
3 - 5 years	3.80	(19)
6 - 10 years	3.80	(5)
11 or more years	4.42	(12)
	($F = 4.23$, $p < .05$)	
Previous Service: 3 to 9 years		
Expected future service:		
Up to 2 years	3.55	(10)
3 - 5 years	4.06	(22)
6 - 10 years	3.94	(19)
11 or more years	4.32	(49)
	($F = 5.99$, $p < .01$)	
Previous Service: 10 or more years		
Expected future service:		
Up to 2 years	3.83	(3)
3 - 5 years	3.84	(11)
6 - 10 years	4.36	(21)
11 or more years	4.39	(30)
	($F = 2.49$, $p =$ N.S.)	
Total Sample		
Expected future service:		
Up to 2 years	3.60	(24)
3 - 5 years	3.92	(52)
6 - 10 years	4.12	(45)
11 or more years	4.36	(92)
	($F = 12.49$, $p < .001$)	

[a] Data are for Identification Index C.

IDENTIFICATION WITH THE WORK ORGANIZATION INDICES

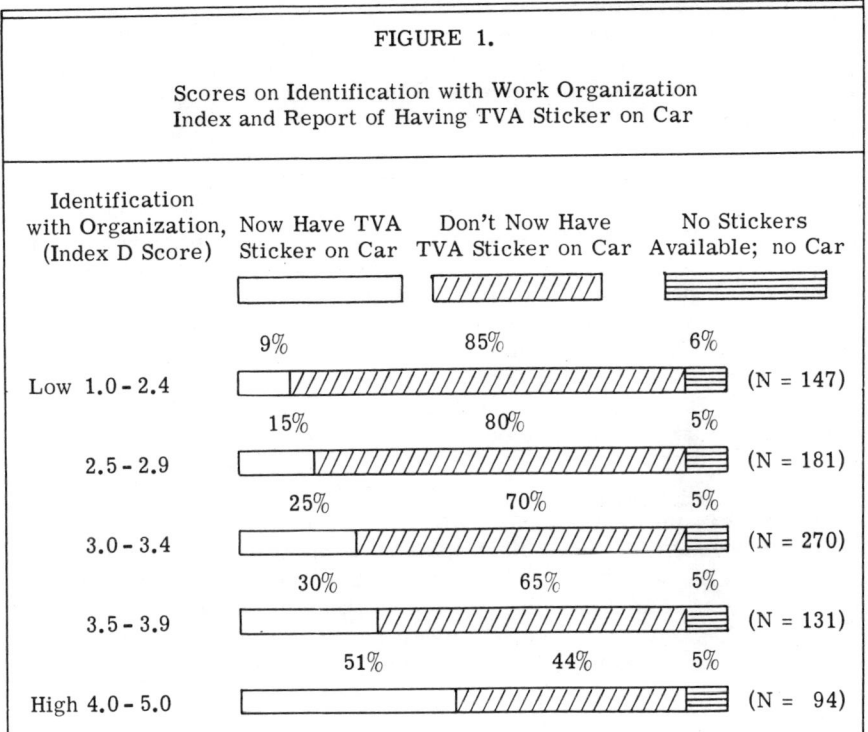

FIGURE 1.

Scores on Identification with Work Organization Index and Report of Having TVA Sticker on Car

always easily available to employees. In any case, over five times as many "high identifiers" as "low identifiers" report displaying these stickers.

Relation to Turnover:

<u>TVA</u>. Turnover among the units studied at TVA occurred primarily in the engineering divisions. Two types of analysis were made: a) a correlation of branch turnover scores with branch identification scores, and b) a comparison of the identification scores of those people who resigned after taking the questionnaire with the scores of those who remained.

For each of twelve branches in TVA engineering divisions, the percentage of employees who resigned over a two-year period (one year preceding and one year following questionnaire administration) was computed from company records. Turnover scores for each branch were then correlated with the mean score on identification with TVA obtained by persons in that branch. The correlations between turnover rates and Identification Index D is close to zero. The expected negative correlation (high identification, low turnover) does occur when Identification Index B is used but the correlation coefficient is quite low ($r = -.23$) and statistically non-significant.

A possible reason for the low size of the correlation is that the turnover rates for each unit may have been greatly influenced by persons whose characteristics were not typical of those in the unit. (The records used did not reveal the job classification or the sex of those resigning.)

In a second type of analysis, a mean was computed for fifteen persons who resigned from Engineering Division 1 (where most turnover occurred) in the year following administration of the questionnaire. The identification index scores of those who left were compared to the mean identification scores of the much larger number (182) in that division who remained with the organization. Those who left TVA had a significantly lower mean score (16.5) on Identification Index D than the mean score (21.4) of those who remained. This difference is statistically significant at the .001 level. A difference of the same level of significance is found when we compare the "leavers" and "stayers" on the shorter Identification Index B.

Electronics Company. As at TVA, two types of turnover data from the electronics company were related to scores on indices of identification with the organization. For eight male units and three primarily female units, rates of turnover during the year prior to questionnaire administration were computed. The relation of these turnover rates to unit scores on the indices of company identification was then examined. As at TVA, the expected negative association between mean identification score and turnover rates did not appear, either for all units or for male and female units taken separately.

A second type of analysis of turnover and identification at the electronics company (similarly to TVA) consisted in comparing the identification index scores of eleven persons who quit or were fired during the year following our questionnaire administration with the scores of those who remained with the company. For this analysis the company was treated as a whole and unit differences ignored.

This time, as at TVA, a significant relation between identification scores and turnover appeared. The average identification score (on Index C) of those who quit or were fired (3.77) was, as expected, substantially lower than the average scores of those who remained with the company (4.12). The difference is statistically significant at the .05 level, using a one-tailed t-test. (The difference between "leavers" and "stayers" on Identification Index B was also significant at the same level.)

Relation to Expectation of Remaining with Organization

While relatively few employees actually left their organization in the year following the questionnaire administration, there are data on many more employees at the electronics company concerning their intentions to remain with the organization. We asked each employee at the electronics company this question:

IDENTIFICATION WITH THE WORK ORGANIZATION INDICES

"How long would you guess you will be working for (name of company) in the future? (Make a rough estimate.)

(1) ____ Less than a year more
(2) ____ One to two years more
(3) ____ Three to five years more
(4) ____ Six to ten years more
(5) ____ Eleven to fifteen years more
(6) ____ More than fifteen years more

Table 26 shows mean scores on the Index of Organization Identification (Index C) for employees who expect to remain with the company for different lengths of time. The data are shown separately for those with differing lengths of past service.

For the sample as a whole, identification scores increase markedly as we move from employees who expect to leave the company soon to those who expect to stay for increasingly longer periods. The difference between mean identification scores for the four "expected future tenure" groups shown is highly significant at beyond the .001 level. (Similar results are found when Identification Index B, rather than Index C, is used.)

The same strong relation between organizational identification scores and expected length of future service is also seen in Table 26 when we look separately at those with up to three years previous service and those with three to nine years previous service. The relation between identification scores and plans to remain with the company is not quite as clear for those with ten or more years service, though it is still apparent. This slight blurring of the relationship is probably accounted for primarily by the fact that the high identifiers with ten or more years service include more employees aged fifty or over than do the lower identifiers.[12] Some of these employees will reach retirement age soon and so, even with the strongest organizational loyalty, cannot forecast eleven or more years of future service.

In presenting these data, we make no statement about the casual direction of the relationship found between identification scores and plans to remain with the organization. Identification may lead to plans to stay, or vice versa, or causation may work both ways. The point here is that we would expect these two factors to go together; the fact that they do provides evidence in support of the validity of the measure of identification. This evidence is consistent with the relationship found between scores on the identification index and actual turnover.[13]

---

[12] Fourteen out of seventeen persons aged fifty or more are in the highest identification category.
[13] Expectations of staying with the organization are much more strongly correlated with the index of organizational identification than with the indices of job motivation, interest in innovation, willingness to disagree with supervisors, and acceptance of change.

Relation to Length of Service

On both common-sense and theoretical grounds, identification with a work organization might be expected to rise as length of service increases — though one would expect this association to be very far from perfect. For TVA Engineering division personnel, scores on identification indices B and D correlate .39 and .31 respectively with length of service. The correlations for operating employees and for non-operating employees in the three steam plants are much smaller, however (all under .10). A greater variation in length of service within the engineering divisions — especially the more frequent presence of relatively new men — may help to explain this discrepancy between engineering divisions and steam plants at TVA.

At the electronics company, the median correlation for nine units between organizational identification and length of service is .33, using Identification Index C. The parallel median correlation using Identification Index B is .20. At the electronics company there is considerable variation in the magnitude of this association.[14]

Relation to Attendance

While a low number of absences is not necessarily an indicator of high identification with the work organization, one might expect some negative association between organization identification and absences. At both TVA and the electronics company there are generally negative (higher identification, less absence) but small and non-significant associations between identification index scores and number of absences.

Relation to Other Variables[15]

To help assess the construct validity[16] of the measure of organizational identification, it is useful to examine the relation of scores on organizational identification to other aspects of the work situation. We expected on theoretical grounds (Patchen, 1964) that organizational identification will increase as influence within the organization increases. At TVA, identification with the organization (TVA) is related strongly to the degree of employee participation in a program of labor-management consultation, the "cooperative program." For eight cooperative programs, each covering a branch or division, average identification scores correlate .75 ($p < .05$) with the percentage of employees who served on the cooperative committee; .94 ($p < .001$) with the per-

---

[14] At both TVA and the electronics company, length of service correlates much more strongly with the index of organizational identification than with the measures of job motivation, interest in innovation, acceptance of change, willingness to disagree with supervisors, and general job satisfaction.

[15] The relationships reported in this section are for a shorter form of index D, composed of Q1, 2, 3 and 4.

[16] See p. 9 for a brief discussion of construct validity.

ceived attention given employee suggestions by the cooperative program; and .80 ($p < .05$) with the amount of information employees report receiving about the program.

It is also of interest to examine the relation of the identification index to other variables of interest, for which no predictions of relation were made. For ninety work groups at TVA, average identification scores[17] correlate .42 with the Acceptance of Job Changes Index, zero with Interest in Work Innovation Index scores, and .33 with scores on the Job Motivation Index A. Measures of average satisfaction with promotion chances and average satisfaction with wages have essentially a zero correlation with organizational identification at TVA. This appears to indicate that the measure of identification is tapping something other than a general mood of satisfaction or dissatisfaction.

Summary and Conclusions

Eight questions were chosen from a larger number of items as showing some validity as indicators of a person's identification with his work organization. Four of these items were asked both at TVA and at the electronics company; three were asked only at TVA; and one was asked only at the electronics company.

The four items used at both sites, as well as the single item used only at the electronics company tend to form a cluster, in the sense of intercorrelating. This is especially true at the electronics company. Three additional items (6, 7 and 8) used at TVA do not show positive correlations with other items. These additional items were, however, included in one index of identification because of their relation to other criteria of validity.

Regarding reliability of the measures, the three item Index B, used both at TVA and at the electronics company, has a test-retest reliability of .69 for individuals and .75 for work units. Index C, which adds one additional item (Q5), has a test-retest reliability of .75 for individuals and .79 for groups. Index D, based on seven items used at TVA, has a test-retest reliability of .71 for individuals and .98 for a small number of work groups. These reliability coefficients — especially for individuals — are somewhat below what would be desirable. It seems probable, however, for reasons discussed in the section on methods, that the coefficients for the reliability of group scores at the electronics company are under-estimates of their true values.

The indices of identification with the organization have positive but modest correlations with supervisors' rankings of employees' "sense of belonging" to the organization. These associations are somewhat stronger at the electronics firm than at TVA. In view of the fact that

---

[17]Identification scores at TVA vary more among work groups (those under same immediate supervisor) than within work groups. F for 90 groups is 1.94; $p < .05$.

this characteristic is difficult for supervisors to judge, the magnitude of these correlations could not reasonably be expected to be much higher.

The strongest evidence of the validity of the measures of identification comes from two sources: a) data on display of a TVA sticker and b) data on actual turnover at both sites and on expectations of leaving at the electronics company.

At TVA, there is a strong relation between scores on the identification indices (especially on the seven-item Index D) and displaying a TVA sticker. Those with the highest identification scores were over five times more likely to report displaying an identifying sticker than were those who scored lowest on the identification index.

At both TVA and the electronics firm, there was little association between unit identification scores and unit turnover. However, there was, in both cases, a significant difference between the identification scores of those specific individuals who left their organizations following completion of the questionnaire and those who remained. At the electronics firm, moreover, there is a strong association between identification scores and the length of time employees expect to remain with the company.

Scores on the identification index were also related in the expected positive direction to length of service in some, though not all, units of TVA and of the electronics firm. There was, finally, only a slight relation between the identification scores and attendance — though this relation was not expected to be strong.

Overall, while the measures presented are rough ones, the evidence suggests that they possess a degree of validity which is sufficient to make them useful for making gross distinctions between those high and low on organizational identification. Data on Index B was presented primarily because it was the only common measure available for both sites. However, Index C appears to be superior to Index B — especially with regard to reliability. Indices C and D are hard to compare since they were used in different sites. While the additional items of Index D (those not appearing in Index C) do not correlate well with Index C items, the extra items found in Index D may add to the predictive power of the identification measure.

IX. OVERALL EVALUATION OF THE MEASURES

Before evaluating the measures of employee morale and motivation presented in this report, it is worth noting some evidence that measurement development efforts of this kind are sorely needed. In all, we tried out a total of about fifty-five questionnaire items, each of which was intended to measure one of the five aspects of employee morale and motivation. Twenty-seven of these items, or about half, were discarded at some stage of our work as inadequate. Sometimes an item was dropped because there was not enough variation in responses to it, but most of the discarded questions were found wanting because they showed little evidence of validity against the outside criteria we used. Job motivation proved particularly hard to measure. If we had not been assessing systematically the validity and reliability of items, many items which we now believe are not good measures might have been used on the basis of their face plausibility.

The reliability of the indices, while somewhat below what would be desirable, is within a range which seems to us to be acceptable at this early stage of developing measures of this type. Reliabilities of the measures are somewhat higher for group averages than for individuals, evidently reflecting a tendency for random individual fluctuations to cancel each other out.

In assessing evidence bearing on the validity of the questionnaire indices, it is important to remember that there are no real good criterion measures against which our questionnaire measures can be compared. We have no way of learning the extent to which such data as supervisors' judgments, or performance data, or attendance, or turnover, are accurate indicators of various aspects of morale and motivation. We do, however, have reason to expect at least a moderate agreement between such outside indicators of behavior and the questionnaire indices. In general, the extent of association with validating data is fairly encouraging and does not compare unfavorably with the validity data for many widely used tests of personality and aptitude.[1] At the same time, some of the correlations with validating evidence are low enough to caution us that these measures are far from being precise ones.

The indices appear to be most useful in detecting fairly gross differences in motivation and morale. This is indicated first by the greater agreement of the indices with supervisors' rankings in units where employees vary most on the qualities being measured. It is

---

[1] See, for example, the validity data for scales of the California Psychological Inventory (Gough, 1957) and the review of validity evidence on scales of the Minnesota Multiphasic Personality Inventory (Buros, 1959).

indicated also by the fact that where groups differed widely both in absence rates and in job motivation index scores, there were sizable correlations between group index scores and group absence. Finally it is indicated by sizable differences on the questionnaire indices among those in widely different work settings — e.g., the widely different job motivation scores of production workers as compared to salesmen and the widely different scores of identification with the work organization for those in divisions where employees actively participate in decision-making as compared to units where there is much less participation. Where variation in the characteristics being measured is small — e.g., within some branches with a fairly homogeneous work force — the index measures (and perhaps the validating evidence too) appear to be too rough to distinguish small variations in job motivation, acceptance of change, etc.

As noted elsewhere in this report, there was generally more variation among work groups than within work groups on the indices of motivation and morale. The only exception was on the willingness to disagree index, on which there was appreciable variation both among groups and among individuals within groups. These results concerning variation suggest that the questionnaire indices will often be most useful in comparing organization units, rather than individuals, on the several aspects of motivation and morale. Such unit comparisons will often be of great interest both to researchers and to practitioners. Moreover, in cases where persons will not answer frankly without being assured of individual anonymity (as where a company conducts its own survey), unit comparisons will be the only ones practically possible.

It seems probable that the measures are applicable in a wide variety of work settings. The questions were originally designed to be general enough to apply to a fairly wide variety of jobs at TVA — including professionals, technicians monitoring automated equipment, and craftsmen. The same questions appeared to work well in an electronics company which included some of the same kinds of jobs we had encountered at TVA, but also some new ones such as production workers and salesmen. However, when considered for use in new settings, it would be well to try to assess again (perhaps with the aid of pre-tests) whether all of the questions are relevant in the particular site.

It should be emphasized again that the questionnaire indices presented in this report represent a fairly rough type of measurement. Improved measures of these employee qualities and of other such qualities are desirable. For the present, however, these measures appear to represent a step forward. It is hoped that they will prove useful both to researchers and to practitioners.

LIST OF APPENDICES

A. Answer Sheets For Supervisors' Judgments of Subordinates

B. Procedure Used For Assigning Scores To Employees According To How They Were Ranked By Supervisors

C. Extent of Agreement Among Supervisors in Ranking Subordinates: Percentage Of Employees Who Were Ranked By Different Supervisors Within Acceptable Range of Agreement on Each of Five Characteristics

D. Correlations Among Scores Assigned to Employees on Five Characteristics On the Basis of Supervisor Rankings

E. Correlations of Individual Scores on Questionnaire Indices

APPENDIX A

Answer Sheets For Supervisors'
Judgments of Subordinates

Code number of Judge:_____

Sorting out people to judge

As a first step, go through your deck of cards, and if you feel that you do not know a person or his work well enough to make an informed judgment, set his card aside. Your judgments should be based on what you have observed of the man or his work on the job, and not just on hearsay.

Omit yourself.

If you are not sure whether you know enough about the person to rate him, keep his card. You can always decide later to leave him out.

Qualities to be judged

The Michigan man will discuss the meaning of each of these, one at a time:

    A. <u>Concern for Doing a Good Job</u>

    B. <u>Looking Out for New Ideas</u>

    C. <u>Willingness to Disagree with the Supervisor</u>

    D. <u>Willingness to Take Responsibility for Difficult Jobs</u>

    E. <u>Sense of Belonging to TVA</u>

    F. <u>Acceptance of Changes</u>

Sample Page: Instructions for Judges

Looking Out for New Ideas

a. Refer to your definition card, and *sort* the name-cards into piles.

    In pile 1 put those persons who seem to be *most on the lookout for new ideas:*

Pile 1

APPENDIX A 75

Pile 2

Pile 3

Pile 4

Pile 5
(if necessary)

> In your last pile above put those persons who are *least on the lookout for new ideas* (even though they might be good workers).

---

b. You may have 3 or more piles (the number of piles can be different from the number you used before).
c. Do not let one pile contain more than one-third of your cards.
d. After you have sorted, *write the code numbers* of each person *between the lines above* for his pile.
e. If you lack information about a person on quality B, write his number below:

Can't rate on
this quality:

---

f. Now *mix up* all the cards.

PLEASE TURN PAGE AND GO ON TO QUALITY B.

APPENDIX B

Procedure Used For Assigning Scores to Employees According to How They Were Ranked By Supervisors

TVA. At TVA, scores for ranking by supervisors on a given characteristic (X) were assigned to employees in the following way:

(1) An employee (Employee 1) was given a score representing his percentile standing among the employees ranked on characteristic X by the first judge (Judge A). An example should help to make clear how these percentile scores were calculated. Suppose Judge A has divided twenty employees into four groups with regard to their standing on characteristic X and has placed Employee 1 in the second (next to highest) group. Fifty percent of the employees ranked by Judge A on characteristic X fall below those in group 2, while 25 percent of employees ranked by this judge are above group 2. In other words, those in group 2 fall between the 51st and the 75th percentiles. The percentile score for those in group 2 is arbitrarily set as the mean of this percentile range — i.e., at the 63rd percentile. Employee 1 thus gets a percentile score of 63 representing his ranking score by one judge on characteristic X.

(2) If only one supervisory person ranked Employee 1 on characteristic X, no score was assigned to Employee 1 on characteristic X.

If two supervisory persons ranked Employee 1 on characteristic X and the scores from these two judges are within 50 percentile points of each other, the average of the percentile scores derived from the two judgments was assigned to Employee 1 for characteristic X.

If three supervisory persons ranked Employee 1 on characteristic X and the lowest computed percentile score is within 50 percentile points of the highest score, a mean percentile score, based on the three judgments, was assigned to Employee 1.

Similarly, when three out of four judges, four out of five, five out of six, five out of seven, or six out of eight judges ranked Employee 1 on characteristic X in such a way that the lowest and highest percentile score are within 50 percentile points of each other, a mean percentile score based on the several judgments was assigned to Employee 1.

The procedures described were repeated for each individual on each of the characteristics ranked by judges. As a result of this process, many employees were assigned a "ranked" score on some characteristics but not on others.

Scores representing supervisors' rankings which were computed by the above procedure make up the data used in tables of this report which show the correlation of supervisors' rankings with index scores.

APPENDIX B

Electronics Company. At the electronics company the same general procedure for computing supervisors' ranking scores was followed. The main difference was that a more stringent standard of agreement among supervisors was adopted. Thus, where two supervisors ranked Employee 1 on characteristic X, the two rankings had to be within 30 percentile points in order for the scores to be averaged and be included in the data. Similarly, three supervisors ranking the same employee on the same characteristic had to all be within a 30 percentile points range. Where there were four supervisory judges, 3 out of 4 had to be within the 30 percentile range; 4 out of 5 supervisors had to be within a 40 percentile range; 5 out of 6 supervisors, 5 out of 7, and 6 out of 8 had to be within a 40 percentile range. Where these criteria were met, the scores of all supervisors who ranked the individual were averaged.

Supplementary Procedure at TVA. Supervisory ranking data at TVA was re-processed using the more stringent standards of agreement used at the electronics company. Supervisory scores representing lesser agreement among judges were omitted and new correlations run between supervisory ranking scores on certain characteristics and questionnaire indices of these same characteristics. Results did not differ appreciably from the correlations obtained previously when a less stringent standard for accepting judges' rankings was used. Data presented in the report are those using the original (less stringent) standard for accepting judges' rankings which is described above in the TVA section.

APPENDIX C

Extent of Agreement Among Supervisors in Ranking Subordinates: Percentage of Employees Who Were Ranked by Different Supervisors Within Acceptable Range of Agreement,* on Each of Five Characteristics

	Concern For Doing Good Job	Looking Out For New Ideas	Willingness To Disagree With Supervisors	Sense of Belonging To Organization	Acceptance of Changes
TVA					
N of Employees with 2 or more rankings	515	505	499	504	487
Percentage whose rankings meet criteria of agreement	78%	73%	75%	70%	67%
ELECTRONICS COMPANY					
N of Employees with 2 or more rankings	123	115	112	69	97
Percentage whose rankings meet criteria of agreement	70%	75%	71%	68%	68%

---

*See Appendix B for description of criteria of agreement among supervisors. Data reported in this table are based both for TVA and the electronics company, on the procedure used at the electronics company — that demanding close agreement among supervisors.

APPENDIX D

Correlations Among Scores Assigned to Employees on Five Characteristics
On the Basis of Supervisor Rankings

TVA[a]

	Concern For Doing A Good Job (1)	Looking Out For New Ideas (2)	Willingness To Disagree With Supervisors (3)	Sense of Belonging to TVA (4)	Acceptance of Changes in Job Situation (5)
(1)	X	.72	.16	.61	.66
(2)		X	.52	.55	.51
(3)			X	.10	-.15
(4)				X	.60
(5)					X

Electronics Company[b]

	Concern For Doing A Good Job (1)	Looking Out For New Ideas (2)	Willingness To Disagree With Supervisors (3)	Sense of Belonging to Electronics Co. (4)	Acceptance of Changes in Job Situation (5)
(1)	X	.81	.69	.65	.44
(2)		X	.81	.48	.50
(3)			X	.22	.29
(4)				X	.63
(5)					X

---
[a] N for TVA correlations is approximately 350.
[b] N for Electronics Company correlations ranges from 30 to 66.

APPENDIX E

Correlations of Individual Scores on Questionnaire Indices

TVA (N = 834)

	Job Motivation Index A (1)	Interest in Work Innovation Index A (2)	Acceptance of Job Changes Index (3)	Identification with Work Organization Index B (4)	Willingness to Disagree Index A (5)
(1)		.21	.30	.36	.05
(2)			.18	.09	.36
(3)				.37	-.02
(4)					.01

Electronics Company (N = 223)

	Job Motivation Index B (1)	Interest in Work Innovation Index A (2)	Acceptance of Job Changes Index (3)	Identification with Work Organization Index B (4)	Willingness to Disagree Index B (5)
(1)		.34	.08	.28	.24
(2)			.24	.00	.52
(3)				.31	.06
(4)					.02

REFERENCES

American Psychological Association, Committee on Psychological Tests, *Technical Recommendations For Psychological Tests and Diagnostic Techniques.* Washington, D.C.: APA, 1954.

Bechtoldt, H.P. "Construct Validity: A Critique," *American Psychologist, 14,* 1959, pp. 619-629.

Blauner, R. *Alienation and Freedom: The Factory Worker And His Industry.* Chicago, Ill.: The University of Chicago Press, 1964.

Buros, O. K. (Ed.) *The Third Mental Measurements Yearbook.* New Brunswick, N.J.: Rutgers University Press, 1959.

Campbell, D. T. and Fiske, D. W. "Convergent and Discriminant Validation By the Multitrait-Multi-Method Matrix," *Psychological Bulletin, 56,* 1959, pp. 81-105.

Campbell, D. T. and Tyler, B. "The Construct Validity of Work-Group Morale Measures," *Journal of Applied Psychology, 41,* 1957, pp. 91-92.

Campbell, D. T. "Recommendations For APA Test Standards Regarding Construct, Trait, or Discriminant Validity," *American Psychologist, 15,* 1960, pp. 546-553.

Carlson, R. E. et. al. *The Measurement of Employee Satisfaction.* Industrial Relations Center, University of Minnesota, 1962.

Coch, L. and French, J. R. P., Jr. "Overcoming Resistance to Change," *Human Relations, 1,* 1948, pp. 512-532.

Cronbach, L. J. and Meehl, P. E. "Construct Validity in Psychological Tests," *Psychological Bulletin, 52,* 1955, pp. 281-302.

Decker, R. L. "A Study of Three Specific Problems in the Measurement and Interpretation of Employee Attitudes," *Psychological Monographs, 69,* no. 16, 1955.

Ebel, R. L. "Must All Tests Be Valid?" *American Psychologist, 16,* 1961, pp. 640-647.

Edwards, A. L. *Manual, Edwards Personnel Preference Schedule,* Revised 1959. New York: Psychological Corporation, 1959.

Ghiselli, E. "The Forced-Choice Technique in Self-Description," *Personnel Psychology, 7,* 1954, pp. 201-208.

Ghiselli, E. "The Validity of Management Traits in Relation to Occupational Level," *Personnel Psychology, 16,* 1963, pp. 109-113.

Gough, H. *Manual, California Psychological Inventory.* Palo Alto, Calif.: Consulting Psychologists Press, Inc., 1957.

Lodahl, T. and Kejner, M. "The Definition and Measurement of Job Involvement," *J. Applied Psychology,* In Press.

Macauley, D. A. et. al. "Cornell Studies of Job Satisfaction: Convergent and Discriminant Validity for Measures of Job Satisfaction by Rating Scales," Cornell University, 1963, Unpublished manuscript.

Mahoney, G. M. "Unidimensional Scales for the Measurement of Morale in an Industrial Situation," *Human Relations, 9,* 1956, pp. 3-26.

O'Connor, P. and Atkinson, J. W. "The Development of an Achievement Risk Preference Scale: A Preliminary Report," Department of Psychology, University of Michigan, 1960 (mimeo).

Patchen, M. "Labor-Management Consultation at TVA: Its Impact on Employees," *Administrative Science Quarterly,* In Press.

Patchen, M. "Participation in Decision-Making and Motivation: What is the Relation?" *Personnel Administration, 27,* 1964, pp. 24-31.

Roach, D. E. "Dimensions of Employee Morale," *Personnel Psychology, 11,* 1958, pp. 419-431.

Sherif, M. and Cantril, H. *Psychology of Ego-Involvements.* New York: John Wiley and Sons, 1947.

Willerman, B. "Group Identification in Industry," Unpublished Ph.D. dissertation, Massachusetts Institute of Technology, 1949.